Shorelines of America

Books by Irwin Stambler

BUILD THE UNKNOWN
A GUIDE TO MODEL CAR RACING
THE WORLD OF MICROELECTRONICS
THE WORLDS OF SOUND
SHORELINES OF AMERICA

Shorelines of America
By Irwin Stambler

A W. W. NORTON BOOK

Published by
GROSSET & DUNLAP, INC.
A National General Company
New York

COPYRIGHT © 1972 BY IRWIN STAMBLER

LIBRARY OF CONGRESS CATALOG CARD NUMBER:
71-153925
ISBN: 0-448-21418-0 (TRADE)
ISBN: 0-448-26188-X (LIBRARY)

ALL RIGHTS RESERVED
PUBLISHED SIMULTANEOUSLY IN CANADA

PRINTED IN THE UNITED STATES OF AMERICA

PHOTO CREDITS

The author and publisher wish to thank the following sources for making their photographs available for use in this book:

Florida News Bureau: 4, 155, 162, 166, 169; Massachusetts Department of Commerce and Development: 8, 83, 96; Scripps Institution of Oceanography: 13, 15, 26, 29; Irwin Stambler: 33; Moody Institute of Science: 39; Union Oil Company of California 76 Magazine: 44; Lockheed: 48; Oregon State Highway Department: 53, 63, 67, 71 top; Washington State Department of Commerce and Development: 71 bottom, 75, 78; Maine Department of Sea and Shore Fisheries: 86, 88; Rhode Island Development Council: 99; City of New York: 112; Virginia State Travel Service: 115 top; Maryland Port Authority: 115 bottom; State of South Carolina: 118, 123 top; Texas Highway Department: 131, 138, 144, 147; Port of New Orleans: 134; National Aeronautics and Space Administration: 159 top; Miami Beach News Bureau: 159 bottom.

Cover photo by James Sprague

Contents

1	The Thin Dividing Line	1
2	The Golden Shore	20
3	North of Morro	41
4	The Great Northwest	59
5	The Rockbound Shore	81
6	Mid-Atlantic Coast	105
7	The Gulf Coast	126
8	Land's End	151
	Index	

Recommended Reading

Acknowledgments

A book may be written by one person, but it cannot come to fruition without the aid and encouragement of many people and/or organizations. For this reason, I would like to express my thanks to Kay McArdle, Nelson Fuller and staff members of Scripps Institution of Oceanography, Lockheed Ocean Systems Division, Honeywell Marine Research Laboratories, University of Rhode Island; New Jersey Department of Economic Development, Division of Shell Fisheries; Florida Department of Fisheries; Department of Ports and Terminals of the City of New York; Texas Highway Department; Washington State Department of Commercial and Economic Development; Oregon Economic Development Department; South Carolina Department of Parks, Recreation and Tourism; Maine Department of Sea and Shore Fisheries; Massachusetts Department of Commerce and Development.

IRWIN STAMBLER
BEVERLY HILLS, CALIFORNIA

Chapter 1

The Thin Dividing Line

When an orbiting astronaut looks back at earth, he sees the broad expanse of blue-green ocean around the North American continent standing out sharply from the greens, browns and reddish-browns of the land. But between them he sees something else, a sharp dividing strip that shows up as a very thin white to pink line in the striking color photographs taken by Gemini and Apollo crews during orbital flight. Such a line marks off almost two-thirds of the borders of the United States.

This thin line, almost invisible if the photographs are viewed from a distance, is the fringe of sand that separates the home of man from the hostile world of water. This is the shore.

It is here that a never-ending battle takes place between land and sea, with first one, then the other reclaiming a part of the territory for its own. Whether the region is the rocky coast of New England, the warm coral sands of the Florida peninsula or the surfer's paradise along the shore of southern California, the battle generally takes the same form. But the combating elements change somewhat from one place to another. The particles that make up the shoreline, for example, may come from sources that are widely different in shape, location and makeup. The currents of the ocean may bring varying temperatures to the attack or different levels of force to bear. And the life forms that exist in this marginal zone, the plants and inhabiting animals, are often peculiar to the conditions of a particular region, and may be very different from those of another.

It is true that the countless pioneers who crossed America to found a new nation paid little attention to these variations in themselves. Even today there is not much notice taken of them by the people who live in the great cities that loom large on the skyline above many a stretch of beach. But whether man realizes it or not, the nature of the shoreland has had its effect on him. Obviously, the conditions at the sea's edge were a major factor in many an early explorer's decision to land or sail on. And the formation of the shoreline—whether it was straight and unprotected, rocky and forbidding, or sharply indented to form a natural harbor—had a great deal to do with the eventual location of a major settlement.

The conditions of the shore affect life around it more subtly as well. Some of man's living patterns in major coastal regions of the nation can be related to the conditions of the area. For example, the kinds of homes men built obviously depended partly on the corrosive effects of the sea air, the temperature along the land-sea boundary and the kinds of vegetation in the vicinity. Even today, when advanced technology has brought a great deal of conformity to construction, cultural approaches and living habits across the nation, there is still a feeling of variety from one shore to another. Los Angeles and San Francisco are different from each other in tone and appearance, and neither would be mistaken for Miami, Charleston or New York.

The shore itself also acts as a magnet for a good share of the population. The rush of new immigrants to America has slowed to a trickle compared to the massive influxes of the last century, but it still goes on. Many thousands still approach America's shores from abroad and most of these newcomers still take root at first in seaport cities. There they join an already sizeable percentage of Americans who live near the sea and earn their living from the ebb and flow of sea-based commerce. So though the entire length and breadth of the nation has been conquered and settled, the largest concentration of population still remains on or near the coastline, accounting for something like 50 percent of the entire population.

Why do people want to stay on the edges of the continent? The economic factor, of course, is an important one. The major share of commerce between nations is still carried on by ocean going vessels. There is also some contribution caused by a certain inertia in man. Once he ar-

The thin dividing line between ocean and shore stands out sharply in this view of Daytona Beach, Florida.

rives at a new destination, he has a natural desire to "sit and rest a spell." This is because, in most cases, a man needs great external pressures to generate enough energy to leave his old homeland. As soon as he reaches his new goal, and the previous pressures are removed, he has a feeling of both relief and exhaustion. This feeling makes him want to settle back into some form of regular routine rather than delve further into unknown and challenging environments.

But perhaps there is a third reason at least as compelling. This is man's deeply felt tie to the sea. Human beings are awed by the restless forces of the ocean and often fear the dangers of the tossing waters. But man is also attracted to them, possibly because of a still remaining thread of memory that connects him to what scientists believe is his ancestral home in the oceans.

Whatever the causes, man has taken up residence in great numbers along the American shores. If the first explorers were to return to these heavily populated sections, they would find them unrecognizable—so much has man changed them. On the other hand, there are places that would seem only slightly different from what they were like hundreds of years ago. To the casual observer, the coast of northern California and Oregon would fall into this class, as would much of the southeastern Atlantic shore and some of the Gulf coast. These sections seem untouched by the expansion of gigantic megalopoli, supercities that cover hundreds of miles along the shore. But even in places where few, if any, men have walked, the appearance of age-old sameness is just an illusion.

Actually, change is the order in almost all things. And nowhere is this more true than along the sea-land boundary. In fact, the most important thing about the shore is its changeability, or impermanence. It does not change occasionally or simply over long periods of time, but ceaselessly. It changes in response to many things—to the movement of the ocean, the beating of rain, the blast of winds, the gravitational forces of the solar system. It is also affected by the actions of man. Direct changes come from building on it— even the beat of footsteps on the shores. Indirect changes can result from alterations in the land and the rivers hundreds of miles inland.

Like the churning waters around them, beaches are not solid, immovable geological formations. Rather, they are long rivers of tiny particles that move and flow just as the particles of water in the ocean currents do.

Willard Bascom, one of the world's foremost experts on ocean engineering, stresses in *Waves and Beaches* that a beach "is a deposit of material in transit, either alongshore or offshore and onshore. The important thought in the definition is that of motion, for beaches are ever-changing, restless armies of sand particles, always on the move."

You can't see this constant movement in the course of a few hours of watching. But, notes Bascom, "overnight, or after a week, the net effect of the waves may be easily observable. Now you notice that a rock is covered (or uncovered) by sand; you see a small vertical cliff out into the berm[1] or a newly added ridge of sand along the beach face; a little way offshore the waves break in a different place, indicating the bar[2] has shifted. The sand feels different beneath your feet—a new layer of sand, not yet compacted by waves, is soft to walk on. . . ."

Change is the watchword for all shores, and all shores show different types of changes. The beaches in the Pacific Northwest are far different from those of California or New England. The shape of the beaches varies widely from one place to another. Here they may be long and narrow, there short and wide. But the processes by which these changes occur are constant from beach to beach. And the methods by which the beaches form and reform are roughly the same for all regions.

The most important agents for change in the life of a beach are the waves and the water currents. The waves usually are formed by actions in the ocean thousands of miles from the land. Storms or winds set waves in motion, and supply enough energy to keep them going over vast distances. Strangely, though the waves continue to march across large sections of the globe, individual water particles travel very little. Wave action occurs when a group of water particles are started moving in a circular orbit by some kind of oscillation or vibration. The circular motion of the particles causes the next group of particles to rotate, and so on. Thus a long

---

[1] The berm is the elevated, flat or gently sloping section (or the series of sections) that forms the above-water portion of a beach.

[2] A bar is an underwater ridge (underwater, that is, except during unusually low tide conditions) of sand, gravel or other material that parallels the shoreline.

The artistry of the shore is demonstrated by these ripple marks impressed by waves on the beach at Provincetown, Massachusetts.

train of rotating sections of water is started, but the individual particles simply revolve in place.

This rotating movement continues with little loss of energy as long as the wave train is crossing open ocean, and the sea bottom is far below the vibrating surface. As the wave nears the shore, however, and the sea floor comes ever closer to the surface, the shape of the floor starts to affect the wave. One thing it does is to slow the wave down from its previous speed of 15 to 20 miles an hour. This action causes the wave to become steeper, changing the shape of the water particle orbits from circles into ellipses. As the water depth becomes smaller, these ellipses are squeezed together and the crest, or top of the wave becomes more like a point instead of the rounded form it had in the deep ocean.

All of these actions make the wave less stable and more likely to collapse in the form of a breaker. This collapse takes place, scientists have found, when the water depth is about equal to 1.3 times the wave height. When this point is reached, there is not enough water ahead of the advancing wave to make a complete elliptical section of water. Now the oscillating particles reach the top of their orbit with nothing in front to support them. The result is a sudden abrupt fall rather than a completion of a smooth orbit.

If, from this point on, the wave is approaching the end of the sea and the beginning of the beach, the wave will disappear entirely in a last swish of a bubbling water and air mixture called foam. However, the first critical 1.3 wave height depth may be a subsurface stretch of sand called a bar. If it is, the depth may again increase beyond the bar before the beach is finally reached. In this case, the wave will reform, though it will be smaller in size due to the energy lost in breaking, and continue on until it once more collapses, this time forever, on the approaches to the true seashore.

(This pattern holds true for a beach. It does not for another type of shore. Obviously, if there is no gradual slope and the shore consists of cliffs or rocks, as along the coast of Maine or Massachusetts, the wave will keep almost all its energy until it smashes headlong into the obstruction. At this time, tremendous sprays of water can be hurled high into the air, possibly as much as a hundred or more feet above the sea surface. The pounding of the waves, in this case, slowly eats away at the rock, grinding its particles into sand. In time, it sets the stage for the formation of new beaches where once there were none.)

The place where the wave fades and dies is called the surf zone. Sometimes a wave dies with a roar, having lifted sharp crests high into the air that crash down with the sound of thunder over distances of 10 to 20 feet and more. Sometimes, when the overall conditions of weather and sea bottom are different, the wave slides gently to its end in a swirl of foam that washes upward on the beach for a few feet, then slides rapidly back beneath the next line of incoming water.

But whether the wave dies hard or gently, the actual amount of energy present in the surf zone is considerable. The wave picks up a great amount of energy as it comes from its far off point of origin. And this energy, gathered in the journey of a thousand miles and more, must be disposed of suddenly in the hundred or so feet that make up the surf zone. Studies have shown that the intensity of the forces involved in the surf zone is actually greater than that in the storm zone, the area that originally gave birth to the wave.

It is no wonder, then, that the shore is a region of such great movement. The tremendous forces in the surf zone tear at the sand particles beneath the waves and claw at the particles lying just out of reach on the shore. As the gravitational pull of the moon and sun changes, the water is pushed higher and higher on the beach, exposing more and more sections of the land to the onslaught of the sea. Later, as the tides change from high to low, the waves slowly recede, leaving their imprint on the land in the form of a hardly noticeable, yet profound change in the positions of the sand masses.

All of this action has a reaction on the water. The movement of the sand changes the shape of the sea bottom in the surf zone, so that the sand or cobbles may be piled higher in one place, lower in another. With a different shape to the sea bottom, the form the waves take varies. The result may be to compress the wave particles into steeper ellipses, making them more unstable and likely to break even more sharply. Or the result may be the opposite.

In all of this turmoil, it is difficult to separate sea from land. In the surf zone, a tremendous amount of sand particles are always in suspension in the incoming water, ready to be deposited on the sea bottom or on the beach, depending on conditions.

There are definite patterns to the movement

of the sand by the ocean. Usually ocean waves reach the land at something like a 30- to 60-degree angle. This results in some sand being carried into the beach in the surf zone in this forward direction and some being carried back down by the receding water after it has washed ashore. As the principles of mechanics show, a force transmitted at an angle is actually the summation of two smaller forces, one vertical and one horizontal. (The forces might be thought of as a right angle triangle, with the angled force as the hypotenuse.) Thus the wave action sets up two forces, one at right angles to the shore and one parallel to it. The latter force sets up a current through the surf zone called a longshore current, which carries great amounts of sand with it and has a major effect on the beach process, as we shall see in our discussion of the submarine canyons off southern California.

It is the longshore current, too, that causes riptides, which can be so frightening and dangerous to amateur swimmers. They occur because the water flowing parallel to the shore eventually has to return to the ocean, which means it has to break through the incoming waves at some point. This happens when the sea floor topography, the physical structure of the sea bottom, combines with a change in the wave pattern that allows the longshore flow to break through and return to sea. This return current, or rip, is usually allowed only a narrow gap in the wave system to use as a return corridor. To get through this narrow opening, the water from the longshore current must speed up. This results in a very strong flow that can take an unwary swimmer out beyond the surf zone rapidly.

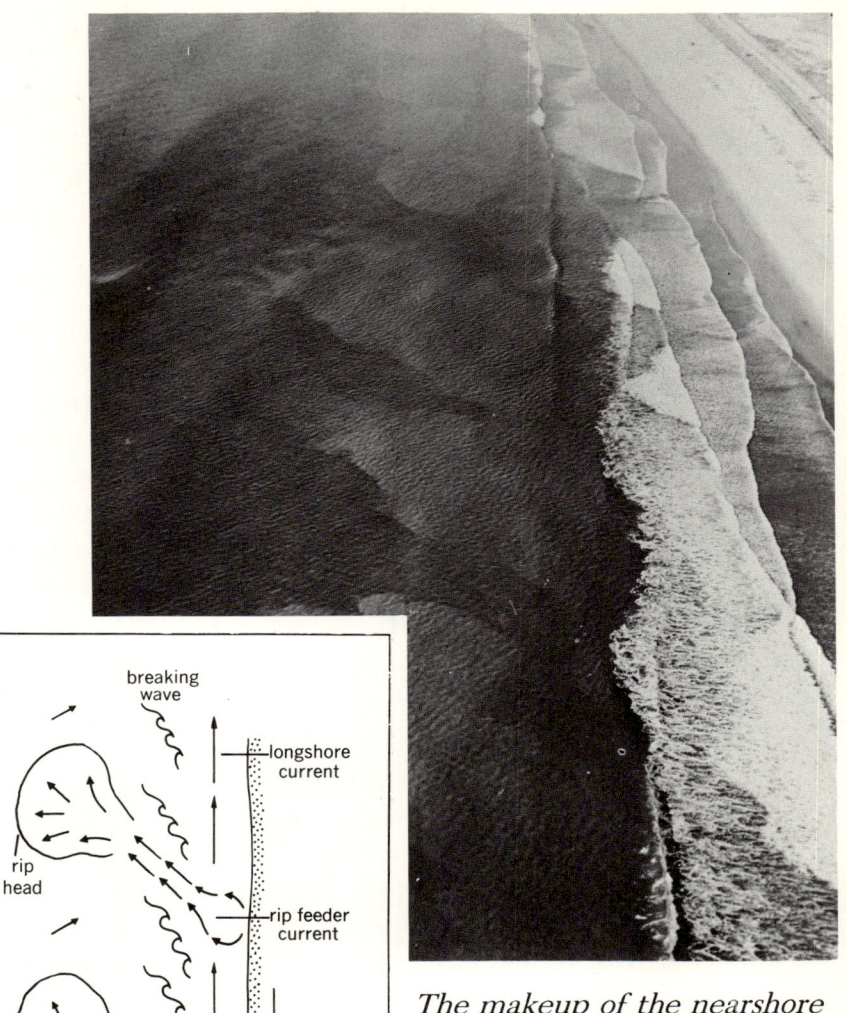

The makeup of the nearshore current system, indicated in the diagram, is clearly evident in the picture of rip currents taken by Scripps Institution scientists. Dark colored tracer chemicals were placed in the water to bring out the regular spacing of the rip currents.

Because the rip current is narrow, though, all a swimmer usually has to do to escape is to swim just a little bit to one side or the other. He then is in the wave movement toward shore and can return just by relaxing and moving with the surf.

Not only does the wave system shape the ocean, it is constantly reshaping the beach like a giant sculptor, lifting billions of tiny sand grains every moment and setting them down in new positions. Thus, trillions upon trillions of sand grains are raised and lowered, moved onshore or taken beneath the waves every second along some 4,000 miles of American shoreline. Yet for all that, cross sections through most of these regions would show that beaches have the same general kind of features. Scientists who study the shore have given names to most of these features.

The beach or shore is considered to extend from the lowest water line to the highest point reached by the waves at high tide. The region that stretches inland from the point of the highest wave is called the coast. The region that stretches seaward from the low water level point is called the offshore. The beach or shore is considered to consist of two parts. From low water level point to the maximum landward point reached by the final uprush of a dying wave is called the foreshore. The backshore is the region between the latter point and the coast. The height of the sand in the backshore is called a berm. The backshore may consist of one long, flat or sloping berm or a series of varying-level smaller berms.

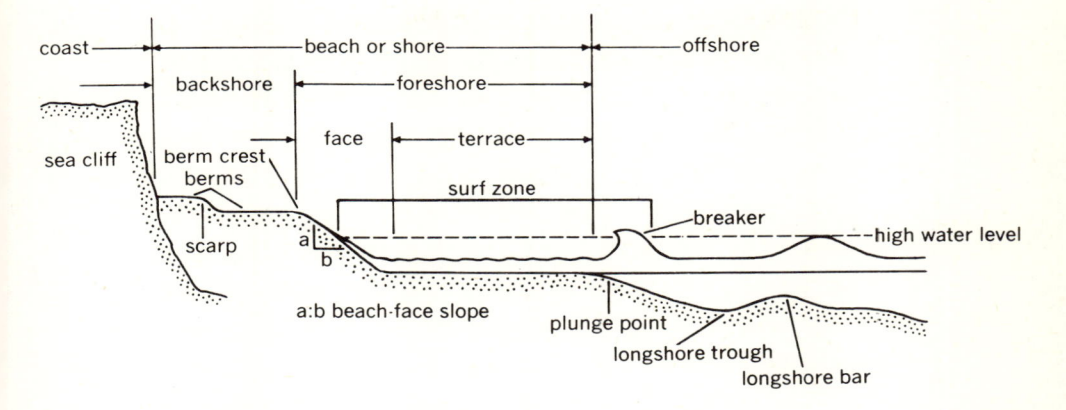

Major features of the shore are indicated in the diagram composed by Dr. Douglas Inman of Scripps Institution.

As the waves move in along the foreshore, they usually break along a gently sloping part of the sea floor called the terrace. For the last few feet, though, the uprush climbs a much steeper beach section that is called the face.

As Professor Douglas L. Inman of Scripps Institution of Oceanography states in "Shore Processes" (McGraw Hill *Encyclopedia of Science and Technology*), "Wherever there are waves and an adequate supply of sand or coarser material, beaches form. Even man-made fills and structures are effectively eroded and re-formed by the waves."

How do beaches form? The first step is the sorting out of material. Coarse material remains on the beach and fine material is carried away by the water. At the same time that this sorting action takes place, the material used to form the beach is rearranged. Some of it is "piled high above the water level by the uprush of the waves to form the beach berm, some carried back down the face to form the foreshore terrace."

Where does the material used to form the beach come from? Some, of course, is gained by the erosion of the waves as they continuously chip away at solid coastlines. But in most regions, the major portion of the beach material is brought to the ocean from inland. The rains that beat on the land cause soil or rocks to move into streams and rivers. The rivers in turn erode away the rocks and move the fine particles toward the sea along with soil particles. The distances traveled by the particles may be great. The mighty Mississippi, for example, is brown and muddy looking along most of its length, demonstrating that a great amount of soil from the heartland of America is constantly brought to it by its tributaries. Indeed, from the far northern borders of mid-America, even from regions of Canada, particles of the land ceaselessly flow into the Mississippi for the long thousand-mile journey down to the Gulf of Mexico.

In the same way, the rivers of the east and west, north and south, carry their share of land to join the turbulent shore regions from Mexico to Canada on the Pacific coast and from the Everglades to Maine on the Atlantic.

Thus the building of the shores takes away from the land in a worldwide cycle of change and regeneration. It is not all a one-way street, however. If it were, the world would be a huge ocean. To balance the forces of nature, new sections of land are thrust up by means of earthquakes or other violent change. The forces in the shore regions themselves contribute to the balance by sometimes causing a gradual rise of land offshore that traps incoming soil and sand. A new island is steadily built in that way. Eventually, the sea that lies between that island and the shore is forced out and replaced with a small valley.

These effects, however, take decades or centuries. In the meantime, the sea has its way with the shore, shaping it to widely different contours as the seasons change and the tides continue their ceaseless fluctuation.

The most striking difference in the nature of the shore can be seen by comparing the summer and winter beach. In winter, the berm, the height of the sand in the backshore, becomes narrower and narrower, even seeming to disappear altogether in some regions. In the summer, the berm seems to grow. It is as if it does so to provide a place for man to spend his leisure time and to enjoy the vistas of the sea.

If you were to compare the winter and summer beach side by side, you might wonder why the sand would be so completely depleted in winter. Where does it all go? And how does it reappear in time for summer's pleasure? A look at a cross section of a beach indicates clearly that the sand does not disappear—it simply shifts position. In the summer, the berm is wide and not too high, and the foreshore terrace is long and gently sloping; a bar, if present at all, is usually small. In the winter, the berm grows quite thin and much steeper and, just beyond the surf zone, the sand builds up in the form of an offshore bar. Thus the winter sand is actually in hibernation, as it were, waiting for a change in the wave pattern so it can return to build up the berm in summer.

The basic reason for the beach change is the beginning of the fierce storms of winter in the deep ocean regions. These storms send huge waves tumbling toward land, one on the heels of the other. The waves hit the shore with much greater force than those of summer, causing tremendous turbulence, and churning the sand into clouds of water-suspended particles. The closeness of the waves quickly causes all the spaces between the sand grains inside the berm to be filled with water until there is no more room for liquid. When the new waves arrive and break, the water has no place to go but back to the ocean. And it carries a layer of sand back to the sea with each trip. Then in the surf zone, the returning water meets and collides with the current that is moving towards shore. This collision causes the suspended sand to drop to the sea floor, building up the bar.

In summer, the reverse is true. The waves are gentler and further apart. The currents set up by these waves pick up the sand grains from the bar and move them shoreward. The relative infrequency of the waves and the growing warmth of the summer sun dries out the berm. There is room for some of the incoming waves to sink in and leave their sand on the top of the berm. Besides this, the gentler motion of the waves avoids the rapid return rush from the beach. This lessens the friction of the shore and allows the sand particles to slow down until many come to rest on the beach.

While all this is happening, man goes about his business on land, worrying little about the conditions in this vibrant region. But for many life forms, a life-and-death struggle is taking place. As naturalists know, many life forms do exist, and in surprising numbers, in the seemingly empty reaches of the shore. Many animals and microscopic plants have added to the wonder of existence by learning to make their peace and survive in these regions. Others, in places such as the shores of Florida, have helped create the shore itself through their own deaths.

Chapter 2

The Golden Shore

ONE OF THE most fabled shores in America stretches in a shallow arc from just below Morro Bay on the central California coast down to the Mexican border. Warmed by a southerly sun and protected from severe temperature changes by warm and placid offshore currents, the shore of southern California has become a magnet to people from all parts of the nation in the twentieth century.

Until recent years, the shores of this region were almost virgin territory. Only a few small towns broke up the vast areas of farm or ranchland based on old Spanish land grants. Though it remained sparsely populated well into the twentieth century, the long stretch of pink sand fronting the breakers of the Pacific was observed and penetrated by many explorers long before parts of the East coast were studied and settled. A scarce 30 years after Columbus planted Spain's flag in the new world, in fact, Spanish captains sailed along this coast, remarking on the kindly climate and the beautiful coves and headlands that could be found all along the way.

The fact that the region flew the flag first of Spain and then of the Republic of Mexico helps explain the slow rate of change. Spanish colonizers to the North American continent were few and found more than enough to occupy them in the gold-rich regions of Central and South America. The international border also prevented English-speaking settlers from coming in from the east. In the 1800s, of course, with the seizure of California from Mexico by the United States and the discovery of gold near Sacramento in 1848, the picture began to change.

But the shoreline still was left mainly to the waves and the shifting sands because distance and the barrier of the Rockies made the region unattractive for industry. Then the technology of the twentieth century brought the region "next door" to the rest of the country. With the advent of mass air travel in the years after World War II, the steady trickle of newcomers to California turned to a flood. By the mid 1960s, California became the most populated state in the entire United States.

The largest percentage of the newcomers to California headed for the shore, and construction throughout the region boomed. Buildings went up from the headlands just above the beaches to the fringe of low-lying mountains and hills that usually rise up a mile to some tens of miles inland from the ocean. When seen from a plane today, the shore from Tijuana, Mexico, to the city of Santa Barbara, roughly 250 miles north, seems lined by a continuous file of buildings.

One result of all this construction was a drastic change in the skyline from its early natural state. But the topography of the shore has also been drastically altered. California fish and game officials reported in 1970 that the building of dozens of small boat marinas had reduced the acreage of marshes and mudflats, the favored home of many kinds of tidal life, from 330,000 for the entire California coast to only 102,000. Of that, only 12,000 acres is in southern California.

The lust for beach living also made it difficult for the majority of people even to get past the endless rows of houses to observe the remaining areas of beach. Philip Fradkin, a *Los Angeles Times* staff writer, wrote in October, 1969, of a family who came from Iowa to swim in the Pacific Ocean. "They never did. It was impossible to find a camping space near the water.... Millions were vying for the same beach space. The family was able to catch only fleeting glimpses of the blue from behind homes, stores, oil wells, smoke stacks, trees, utility poles and freeway railings...."

According to a *Los Angeles Times* survey, the coastline of California is a dwindling natural resource. And it will continue to shrink as more and more people—not only from the state but from a large part of the nation—flock to it. The more people seek out the sea, the more limited access to it becomes.

What would you see if you were to survey the

coastline by plane, section by section? Halfway between San Diego and Santa Barbara is a dense concentration of buildings. Row after row of small houses, pierced here and there by a few towers of new high-rise buildings, lie right along the shore, almost where the blue water laps the pink sand frontier. Clustered behind some beach sections are groups of low, squat, large rectangular structures. These are the many factories that turn out planes, missile parts, surfboards and other items that support over eight million people in a region that was practically deserted in 1900.

On a clear day the Los Angeles basin is seen to be a roughly bowl-shaped area hemmed in by a ring of blue-black mountains. These mountains trap the incoming fog that often moves in all along the coast of California, piling it up in dense layers over the City of the Angels and keeping it from the long stretch of desert, once the floor of an inland sea, that lies beyond. The mountains also act to keep the air from moving eastward on static, windless days. This action helps keep Los Angeles sheltered and warm, but it also causes the famed inversion layer that keeps the air from circulating beyond the basin. When this occurs, and there is a massive injection of pollution into the air from cars and factories, what results is the scourge of modern cities—smog.

Stretching northward, a series of gently sloping headlands extend down into the ocean for much of the distance from Los Angeles to Santa Barbara and above Santa Barbara to just below the city of Santa Maria. Much of this region seems unoccupied except for some scattered buildings and a few spider-like steel structures that rise on concrete bases. The reason for the lack of homes and population is not that there is something undesirable or forbidding about these areas. These sections just below Oxnard and about 50 miles above Santa Barbara are government reservations forming the Pacific Missile Range. From launch sites in Point Mugu and Vandenberg Air Force Base, to the north, advanced missiles for the nation's defense are tested and satellites destined for polar orbit sent heavenward. Sometimes, in late afternoon or early evening, a watcher from the shore can see a strange, glowing multicolored trail in the sky, indicating that a powerful rocket is in flight.

Where the headlands fronting this stretch of coast jut point-like into the water, there are usually broad beaches to the north of them. These beaches are often two or three times as deep as the sand barriers that front Los Angeles. They demonstrate what happens when an obstruction blocks the path of a longshore current. The blockage stops the movement of part of the current near the shore, causing its sand cargo to settle out. Eventually this sand fills in the shoreline depression with a deep beach.

The effect of headlands on a beach can be duplicated by man-made obstructions, often with undesired results. This can be seen on the Santa Barbara waterfront, where a long pier is protected by a breakwater placed two miles to the north. The pier provides a marvelous vantage point for seafood markets and fine restaurants. From the windows of the stores or the railings of the pier, customers can watch the ceaseless tug of the tides against the backdrop of the hill-fringed city. The pier also provides fishermen with a place to relax while their lines dangle peacefully in the blue water below.

But the view from above shows that the breakwater has the same effect on the longshore current as the headlands. The longshore current is slowed north of the pier, stopping the southward flow of sand and depositing it as a fingerlike extension of the upper part of the indented city shore. This growing sandspit does provide a shelter for small boats to anchor in a shallow natural harbor. But unless the region is constantly dredged to remove excess sand, the spit would continue to grow until the entire area between pier and spit was one huge beach.

Above Santa Maria, the headlands recede from the shore, leaving a long stretch of straight, flat beach lined by a series of beach towns all the way to Pismo Beach, just south of Morro Bay. North of Morro, the coast becomes increasingly more rugged, and the high, sheer cliffs and towering mountains create some of the most striking shore scenery in the world. But this is the subject for another chapter.

The mechanism that forms and maintains the beaches of southern California is generally the same for the entire stretch of coast. Indeed, all the beaches of California began in the same way. With minor exceptions, the original and natural source of all the sand along a thousand miles of state coastline is the rivers and streams that flow toward the Pacific from the mighty Sierra Nevada mountain chain some 100 to 150 miles inland.

Rolling countryside ending in eroding cliffs near the ocean's edge is the general nature of southern California's shore regions. This view shows the campus of Scripps Institution of Oceanography at lower right.

The few exceptions to this are due to the relatively small amount of cliff erosion in places where the waves can come close enough to grind them down. In general, the amount of cliff erosion in southern California waters is very minor except for the region around La Jolla, a section just north of San Diego. Home to the University of California at San Diego and its major oceanographic center, Scripps Institution of Oceanography, La Jolla is surrounded by steep cliffs. Along the base of these cliffs, wave action has carved out a series of unusual cove beaches, one of the features that made early residents give the beautiful area its name, which means "The Jewel."

The major portion of southern California beaches, however, share a common source. The sand in the waves and longshore currents and the sand resting on the shore is made up of a fairly consistent set of materials as well. By far the greatest constituent of it is the mineral known as quartz. Fully 75 percent of southern California sand is quartz, a material that is the basic ingredient of glass and that provided the crystals for the first successful radio sets. Another 15 percent of the sand is feldspar, while the remaining 10 percent (sometimes as high as 15 percent) consists of heavy minerals and, particularly, pitchblende.

The volume of sand that drifts endlessly in the longshore current is considerable. The net drift past most sections of southern California shore is 200,000 cubic yards a year. In some places, such as the region near the city of Ventura, 60 miles from Los Angeles, the sand flow is estimated at over a million cubic yards a year. This is enough to form a beach that would cover as much area as the sprawling city of Los Angeles.

With such an enormous supply of sand available, there seems little doubt that nature can maintain a fine system of beaches along California's southern coast. Actually, however, these beaches are in constant danger. Most Californians are not aware that they might wake up some morning to find 500 miles of rock and stone instead of pleasant stretches of sparkling sand.

There are two reasons for this: one natural and one man-made. The natural reason concerns a series of submarine canyons. The man-made threat is called flood control.

The existence of tremendous submarine canyons was discovered very recently. Until the mid twentieth century, man knew very little about the shape of the ocean floor beyond a few hundred feet out from the shore. But World War II gave the science of oceanography a great push forward. Funds were provided to train and equip scientists to probe the oceans in order to improve American seapower and defense against enemy submarines. After the war, new instruments, such as powerful sonar probes designed to chart the ocean depths and measuring instruments that could detect deep water properties, gave scientists tools to open up the sea frontier.

In the late 1940s, oceanographers announced the discovery that the ocean floor was far from smooth and featureless. It was as varied as the land. One of the new surprises that came from this work was the fact that only a short distance

The continuing threat to the beaches of southern
California can be seen in this underwater photograph.
It shows sand flowing from the nearshore region into
the mouth of one of the many
underwater canyons off California's coast.

from some of the coastal regions of the United States immense underwater canyons were found, many of them spectacularly larger and deeper than the Grand Canyon of Arizona.

A series of these canyons are present just off the southern California coast. The canyon mouths start roughly an eighth to a quarter of a mile out from the surf zone and the canyons run in a westerly direction for hundreds of miles out into the deep ocean. The first major canyon is found near Point Hueneme, below Santa Barbara. Paralleling it at about 40-mile intervals in a southerly direction is a string of canyons that reaches all the way to the Mexican border and continues on down the length of the long Baja California peninsula.

These canyons act as tremendous siphons that trap the sand flowing in the longshore currents. For instance, much of the sand moving south past Santa Barbara in the longshore current moves into the head of the Hueneme Canyon until it fills it up. For a while, this blocks off the canyon. The sand following along in the longshore current then moves past it until the flow reaches the next canyon mouth. Eventually, however, still undetermined processes cause the sand that has filled the canyon head to flow down into the canyon for hundreds of miles, opening the mouth up for another influx of sand from the longshore current.

To maintain the longshore current sand load, new sources of sand from below each canyon region are required. One source of supply is sand from the beaches that is moved by the incoming waves into the longshore current. However, if this process were to continue, the beach sand would be used up in a relatively short period of time and southern California would be without beaches.

Where, then, does the extra sand come from to maintain the natural balance? The answer, as noted before, is from streams and rivers. But this source is in danger too.

A look at the inland geography of southern California shows many winding stream or river beds. In the summer, though, these are reduced to thin trickles or dry up completely. It is because there is essentially zero rainfall for almost nine months out of the year that California gained the nickname "The Golden State" for its many days of bright sunshine.

When the rains do come, however, they can turn the dry waterways into raging torrents. Within hours, the levels of such rivers as the Los Angeles can rise from a few inches to from 6 to 10 feet. In years past, such sudden flooding caused major disasters to many areas of southern California, sometimes washing homes away and drowning many people. Gradually, man overcame this problem by building upriver dams and controlling downstream movement by cementing over the river and stream beds with large concrete channels. The result has been to cut losses from flooding drastically.

At the same time, though, the flow of soil from the mountains and valleys of inland California has been practically eliminated. At one time, the Los Angeles River carried a great volume of soil down to the sea near Inglewood. This soil used to enter the longshore current to replace lost beach sand all the way south to Newport Beach before the mouth of Newport Canyon, a submarine canyon, drew much of the sand down to the deep ocean.

At the start of the 1970s, this sand loss was not too noticeable along the coast. But the situation was serious, as beach scientists were well aware. Dr. Douglas Inman of Scripps Institution of Oceanography summed up the problem. "The growth of pleasure boating in the 1950s and 1960s led to building of many new marinas where weekend sailors could moor their craft." Construction work along the coast thus released large amounts of sand that made up for the loss in sand from rivers and streams.

"But sooner or later, the dredging of basins for boat harbors will come to an end. Then we will be in for a series of crises in some beach areas. Literally, some of our finest beaches can be out of sand within ten years after major dredging work stops."

Obviously, one way to keep sand in offshore circulation is to continue dredging operations. But this is expensive and the public might not be willing to pay for it once private industry no longer foots the bill. Besides, dredging is useful only as long as there is sand to dig up in harbor areas. With no new sand flowing down to the sea, this source will eventually give out too. A better answer, Dr. Inman points out, might be to dam up some of the submarine canyons so that sand coming down from northern California will not be lost to the ocean floor.

Meanwhile, oblivious to future problems, sunbathers and swimmers flock to the relaxing shore

Much of southern California's shoreline is being reshaped by man for his own pleasures. Here is one section of Marina Del Rey boat harbor in Los Angeles.

in ever increasing numbers while offshore, surfers wait for a good wave.

Southern California is definitely surfing country. The conditions along the coast are excellent for the sport, the waves are the right shape in many locations and the mild climate makes surfing possible the year round. It is no wonder that the American surfing craze got its start in this region. Since the early 1960s residents and vacationers have been drawn to the Pacific shore to pit their skills against the ocean forces. Even youngsters who have never had the chance to come within a thousand miles of a foaming seashore were able to share the excitement and dynamics of ocean movement, thanks to the beat of specialized rock music called surfing music. Pioneered by such groups as the Beach Boys, Jan and Dean and other products of Los Angeles area beach towns, the surfing beat swept the nation in the early 1960s.

The surfer may be able to compare the throbbing refrains of rock music to the thunder of breaking waves as the ocean makes its mark on the land. But he does not want the most dynamic waves for his ride shoreward on his long, slender board. Such waves, called plunging waves by oceanographers, rise too sharply and break too rapidly for the board to gain the lift it needs for a long ride.

The plunging breaker occurs when the sea floor in the surf zone is steep and smooth. Under these circumstances, there is nothing to slow the wave down until it is right at the point where the water depth is not great enough to fill in the crest. The wave retains all its energy until this last moment, then gives it up in a fierce, downward plunge that can send geysers of water 40 or 50 feet high into the air or release a long thin train of white foam that poets have compared to the "white manes of plunging horses."

The surfer, though, wants a different kind of scenery. His delight is a wave that breaks slowly, losing its energy gradually but steadily as it moves shoreward. This spilling wave results when the sea floor slopes gently and is pockmarked with rocks or other protuberances. These things slow the wave down, warping the orbits of the water particles so that the crest tumbles down rather than plunges. Such a spilling wave can take as much as several minutes before it finally disappears. It gives the surfer just the right pattern he needs to stand and ride his board on the face of the wave, and allows him to balance himself with swift steps on the plastic coating until the wave dies out and the board comes to rest in the last upwash of the surf.

The surfing addict probably spends more time at the beach than most residents of the cities and towns along the shore. Yet he is rarely more aware than they of the many life forms that mature, reproduce and die in the tide zone beneath his board or on the seemingly lifeless beach. Certainly neither he nor other nearby residents know that these unseen shore dwellers have drastically decreased in numbers in many shore areas, victims of the continued impact of civilization on these regions.

In their monumental book on Pacific shore life, *Between Pacific Tides,* Edward Ricketts, Jack Calvin and Joel Hedgpeth sadly noted, ". . .

all should be aware that the life of the seashore was never adapted to withstand the pressure of hordes of people; places that once abounded with urchins are barren of them now; the abalone, once a dominant animal of the intertidal regions, is now common only on inaccessible offshore rocks or islands [the still relatively uninhabited channel islands off southern California have good numbers of abalone in their waters;] and the rock scallop Himnites, once common in the lower intertidal, is now a rare animal."

It should not be inferred that the tidal zone is uninhabited, however. Far from it. Literally thousands of kinds of animals and plants exist in the various zones between the uppermost beach, where only occasional spray or storm waves come, and the low intertidal, an area uncovered only rarely when the lowest of the low tides momentarily exposes the sea floor to the full light of day.

Most of the specimens of the southern California and Pacific coast shore have their counterparts along the Atlantic. But there is considerable difference in size and detail between Pacific life and their Atlantic relations. The reason is the overall difference in environment. The Pacific shores are subject to waves coming almost unhindered over vast regions of the ocean while the Atlantic is relatively sheltered. The latter waves are slowed down and gentled by often invisible underwater barriers, submarine reefs and bars, underwater mountain chains and the like. Thus wave shock is of greater importance to the way organisms develop in the Pacific shore than along the East coast.

Life forms found in the various zones between low intertidal and high beach tend to live only in their own definite stretches of territory. Where they live depends on the conditions that are present and the life forms themselves. Some forms can only exist under almost total ocean conditions, such as the low intertidal sunflower seastar, presently considered the largest of this family of animals. The seastar's many long-rayed arms reach diameters of two feet and more, and scientists are still arguing about how it uses the hundreds of tiny tube feet on its underbody to move across sand and rock.

The life in the low intertidal zone is rich and plentiful compared to the high beach. In the latter, only a few species survive, usually those that have almost completed a change from sea to land animal. The high beach inhabitants include different kinds of periwinkles, a burrowing worm called the pill worm, and the beach hoppers that often parade along the beach in great numbers in early morning or twilight. Already beyond this zone and now land dwellers are countless millions of snails. The bane of existence to homeowners far into the heartland of the region, these snails gnaw their way through plants up and down the coast and are responsible for great amounts of damage.

From the high beach to the low intertidal, innumerable kinds of plants and animals are found. There are many kinds of crabs, burrowing worms of all descriptions, sea snails, shrimp of varying size and color, anemones with flower-like structures and waving arms, kelp of infinite variety and much more. The sub-species of just the above groups would take many scientific books to classify and describe in complete detail.

Among the most populous of the Pacific coast life forms in the upper zones of protected outer coast is the small, gray-colored acorn barnacle found clinging to many rock formations. Its relative, peculiar to the southern California region, is the even smaller brown barnacle, *Chthamalus fissus*. Among other members of the mollusk family found in the region are several kinds of limpets, mussels and some members of the clam family. One of the latter that was once an edible delicacy of the area is the bean clam, found from Long Beach southward. Unfortunately, the bean clam has declined in numbers so that there are not enough for commercial food use.

In the intertidal zones live such animals as the giant green anemone. Like the goat, it vents its voracious appetite on almost anything it can reach, and it will send its waving tentacles with their stingers out to snare fish, small crabs, even stones. Winding their way among the kelp and anemones are scale worms and small bug-like chitons of very ancient lineage. And under tidal pool rocks in shore areas from Santa Monica to the Mexican border live pale white ghost shrimps, members of the crayfish family, that can flip their tails to swim backward.

In low intertidal zones still other species can be found. These include the small under-rock *Octopus bimaculoides,* dark red-brown crabs, the light-avoiding *Pilumnus spinohirsutus* crab with a covering of spiny protuberances that makes it look like some form of plant life, the Dungeness crab and many others.

An annual happening in southern California is the "grunion run." Answering the rhythm of the tides and nature's cry, swarms of grunion ride the crest of a wave to the shore to deposit their eggs only after the three nights following the full moon in March, April, May and June.

On open coast sandy beaches where the surf plunges unhampered onto the shore, most of the sea forms are of the burrowing type. The region between Santa Cruz and Pismo Beach is inhabited by such burrowers as the mole crab, razor and pismo clams.

These are just a few of the many non-human dwellers along the lower shores of the Golden State. They are described in far greater detail in *Between Pacific Tides.* But before leaving this region to examine its neighbor to the north, one last strange and legendary resident should be briefly mentioned.

This is the grunion, a small six-inch-long fish of the smelt family. These fish answer the rhythm of the tides with faultless perception, coming to the beach to lay their eggs only on the three nights after the full moon in the months of March, April, May and June.

Going grunion hunting is one of the rarer pleasures of southern California living, and hundreds of thousands of people eagerly listen for word that the grunion are running. Then long strings of cars make their way to the beach by the light of the moon. Campfires are lit on beaches all along the coast and many tents go up on the sands, for hunting the grunion is an all-night task. If the timing is right, and the fish ride the tide onto the wet upper tidal sands, thousands fall prey to the hunters who catch them with nets, hats and even bare hands. Those lucky "fishermen" can often be found roasting their catch over a fire as the first faint rays of dawn show above the eastern horizon.

Chapter 3

North of Morro

Beyond Morro Bay, the California coast changes abruptly. Along the southern shore, it has been low lying, a calm and peaceful stretch of beach that goes with the regional image of perpetual summer. But once past Morro it becomes fierce and wild. A driver on Highway 1, the tortuous, winding coast route, finds himself flanked by sheer cliffs and towering heights that seem to slice the shore completely from the rest of the continent.

The scenery during the daylight hours is spectacular. The ocean stretches out unbroken toward the horizon as far as the eye can see. Near the base of the cliffs, the waves smash endlessly against the land, sending plumes of white spray high above the water and rending the air with a dull throbbing thunder. The land is not one long line but protrudes here and recedes there in a series of rocky inlets. Above the cliff faces, the land slopes upward in a progression of small mountains that, on a clear day, can be seen silhouetted against one another far into the distance. But these slopes are not, in most places, the grassy or relatively bare surfaces of the southern coast. Instead, bushes and trees in wild array march up and down the rills and switchbacks. In many places, these trees surround the winding road so tightly that the sun can't force its way through.

In this manner, the shore continues its sheer winding path for over a hundred miles until the hills finally give way to rolling country again and the traveller comes upon the picturesque town of Carmel, a town with many stuccoed homes and flower gardens. Just before Carmel, though, the highway swings behind some bluffs into a valley behind the shore. Here is the first grove of towering coast redwoods, trees with glowing red-brown coats that were young when Caesar's legions spread the arms of the Roman Empire across Europe.

Between Carmel and Monterey, the shore suddenly juts westward to form a peninsula some 17 miles long and almost as deep. This is the Monterey Peninsula. And one of its most interesting features is the presence of tide pools which can be found along the seaward face at low tide. They occur because the cliffs in this area are generally low and fronted by small beaches and rock. The waves that continually pound the shore erode these rocks, cutting them into ridgelike formations known as wave-cut terraces. When the tide is in, most of the low rock formations and the bowl-shaped depressions the waves have carved are covered with many feet of water. When the tide goes out again, the rocks become barriers that hold small quiet bodies of water in the depressions. These are the tide pools and, at low tide, they are bustling underwater cities, full of colorful plants and sea animals that come from their hiding places to conduct their waking-hour activities.

Two-thirds of the way around the Monterey Peninsula, the land suddenly rises up a little higher, sending an arrow-like body of land into the fierce inrush of the ocean. This is Point Lobos, a national monument that shelters many species of bird and plant life on its surface and offers refuge to sea birds and seals at the base of its rocky heights. Part of this stretch of shore forms a habitat for another of nature's rarities, the California Cypress. These stunted cypress trees, with question-mark-shaped gnarled trunks can be found only in the region around Cypress Point on the Monterey Peninsula.

Monterey, a city rich in history, lies at the beginning of a low-lying curved stretch of bay with gleaming pink-white beaches. The shores of the beach were crossed as early as 1602 by Spanish explorer Sebastián Vizcaíno. His reports helped influence colonists to settle there, a step which eventually made the city the Spanish capital of California.

Apparently government officials found the magnificent scenery, the view of ocean and the mountains to their liking, for Monterey remained the capital under four different flags. Following the Spanish rule, it became the seat of

The trees often assume strange and striking shapes along the coast of central California's Monterey Peninsula.

Mexican government. In 1846, after American settlers raised the Bear Flag of the new California Republic in Sonoma, Monterey still held sway. And it remained the capital briefly in 1850 under the Stars and Stripes after California became the thirty-first state in the Union on September 9.

From Monterey to a little past Santa Cruz, the mountains recede from the coast, leaving room for broad beaches and sloping grasslands. Further north, however, except for the sand beach of Half Moon Bay and the area of low reefs just above it, the coast becomes sheer and rocky again. And it becomes increasingly rugged and forbidding as the shore continues northward until, finally, it is breached by what seems to be a narrow ocean inlet.

For a good part of the year, much of this northern region is covered by banks of fog that move noiselessly in and leave only the tops of mountains or ridges showing above the white mass. This white cover formed a shield that fooled many an early explorer into thinking the coast was impenetrable for well over a hundred miles above Santa Cruz to where the mouth of the Russian River carried clear waters from the Coast Range down to the Pacific. The result was a delay of 200 years in the discovery of what is today one of the most famous water areas of the world, San Francisco Bay.

Juan Rodrigues Cabrillo sailed within hailing distance of the Golden Gate in 1542, but landed only on the Farallon Islands some 35 miles to the west. Sir Francis Drake, the famous English sea dog, cruised the coast of California in the late

1500s, but also missed the narrow opening to the bay. He landed instead in Drake's Bay, roughly 30 miles to the north just below the jagged top of Point Reyes. In 1595, Spanish sea captain Sebastián Rodríguez Cermeño found the same harbor Drake did and renamed the place Puerto de San Francisco after St. Francis. It was this name that was transferred to the now-famous city clustered on the hills just to the east of the sheltering headlands. But the transfer of title had to wait until 1769, when an expedition led by Gaspar de Portola finally discovered the wide waterway lying behind the awesome granite heights.

San Francisco Bay is actually an estuary. That is, it is a mixing zone where fresh waters of the land meet the salty inflow from the ocean. With San Pablo Bay, its northern extension, it forms a great basin where the waters from the Sacramento and San Joaquin Rivers join in their everlasting march to the sea. It is one of a very few estuaries on the entire Pacific coast. In all of California, the only other bay considered to fall into this category is Humboldt.

Protected by twin peninsulas, the lower of which is home for the city of San Francisco and the northern for artist-favored Sausalito, San Francisco Bay has little in the way of surf action although the tides ebb and flow in response to the ocean's rhythm as they do in any part of the world's ocean system. In years past, this protection led to the development of a vital and teeming population of fish, mollusks and other seashore life. But since the shore was taken over by man's dwellings and huge industrial plants, the dumping of pollutants from them has wiped out most of this once-abundant life.

By 1970, the residents of the high-rise buildings and hundreds of small two- and three-story houses that climb up and down the hills of San Francisco were alerted that their bay was in mortal danger. Scientists and reporters alike pointed to the practice of filling in many sections of the lower bay with dirt from construction sites or with refuse to permit new building projects. The continuation of this practice, they warned, threatened to eventually replace a good part of the water with land, turning it into an inland valley. The danger was perhaps not as great to the more industrialized areas on the east bay, such as Oakland and Alameda, but even there voices were raised about the loss to the community of a priceless natural resource.

But the dangers to the San Francisco estuary seem far away to the casual traveller proceeding north above the tossing dark blue waters of the Golden Gate on the most famous bridge in the world. Since 1937, the longest cable-supported suspension structure has provided a link between the closely packed buildings of the city and the still wide open space of Marin County. Turning off the highway and going down to the shore, the visitor moves past Stinson Beach to Duxbury Reef, which Joel Hedgpeth, in *Seashore Life*, describes as "a formation of soft shale, especially fine for boring clams and animals nestling within old borings."

Beyond Duxbury, the shore curves outward past Drake's Bay to Point Reyes, turns back roughly at a 45-degree angle to the base of this

An experimental plane glides past one of the relatively level coastal land formations near San Francisco.

point, then sends a small sliver of land northward to Tomales Point. This point is just a few miles from the protected Dillon Beach at the entrance to a long pencil-shaped body of water known as Tomales Bay. The shallow bottom of Tomales Bay is the home of many kinds of shore life and has been the subject of some of the most famous marine studies made in the Pacific coast region.

Tomales Bay is one of the relatively few places along the coast where oysters are grown. The native oyster of the region, called *Ostrea lurida,* is found in small quantities from central California northward, but it is not commercially interesting until the shores of the far northwest come into view. So the California oystermen import larger oysters from the East coast and Japan and grow them in specially protected beds. Thus low tide in Tomales Bay exposes long lines of closely planted stakes in many sections, stakes put up around clumps of oysters to keep out such enemies as stingrays and angel sharks.

The small sliver of land at Tomales Point aims at Bodega Bay, a small marine bay nestled within the curving grasp of a fist-like headland called Bodega Head. From the sands of Dillon Beach, the view northward shows the coast to consist of a series of headlands that point down to the breaking waves like a series of fingers. Fronting the shallow cliffs along much of the shore are small rises of rock standing like dark sentinels a short distance offshore all the way to the horizon.

This is a shore pattern that continues for much of the rest of the northern California coast, an area that sweeps in a gentle arc for 400 miles from San Francisco past Cape Mendocino to Humboldt Bay near the border of Oregon. The arc of the coast swings out toward the west at Cape Mendocino, then curves back eastward. Though it may be hard to see it on a normal map projection, geographers tell us that this sweep makes Cape Mendocino the point on the continental United States that extends furthest to the west (excluding Alaska).

For the most part, this is still relatively wild, undisturbed country. Only trees and an occasional small town disturb the symmetry of nature. The beaches in this area are somewhat darker than they are below Monterey, reflecting different sources of supply. The sand still comes mostly from the rushing waters moving to the ocean from hills and mountains, but the rocks and stones that have been ground down by wind and water are often different in mineral content from those of the southern coast. The range of colors in the beaches varies widely from one place to another, too. Sometimes the sand is coarse-grained and light-colored, like the beaches all up and down the coast from Point Conception to Mexico. In other cases, the sand may be dark brown, reddish-brown or even gray-black.

The shore life must be able to withstand a considerably different kind of climate here than to the south. For one thing, there are well defined seasons in this northern region, unlike the mild, relatively unchangeable climate of southern California. In the summer it is usually sunny but cool, while the winter months are cold and damp. During the winter, too, the waves are often whipped to a fury by winds that have gathered energy over 7,000 miles of open ocean. They hurl themselves against the shore in a constant procession of thundering reverberations. From fall through spring, steady rains can be expected from time to time, although for the most part the shore here is wetted down by a continuous drizzle or a blanket of stationary fog.

As a result, the coast has far more of the green hues of the East than the desert brown seen on many stretches of southern California coast. The greater rainfall encourages the growth of many kinds of trees, including the rare California Redwood. Groves of these redwoods are found in several places just inland from the coast starting with Muir Woods near Sausalito. In one section at the far northern tip of California just below Crescent City, the towering redwoods of Jedediah Smith State Park can be seen from the surf zone.

Another difference between the northern shore and the southern is the temperature of the water. Here it is much colder, reflecting the flow of a strong current coming down from the north called the Japan Current. This current clashes with the northward-circulating Humboldt, or California Current, a warm water current that flows near Monterey. The collision of these great rivers in the ocean causes a chaotic water state near Monterey, accounting for some of the odd wave patterns that sometimes churn the shore around the Monterey Peninsula.

The main reason for the coldness of the near shore waters is due to a phenomenon called upwelling, however. That is, colder water from the lower layers of the ocean move up to the surface.

Upwelling in this region occurs as follows: The prevailing winds along the northern California coast are from the northwest and are roughly parallel to the shore. The result of this wind action is to drive the surface water westward, approximately at right angles to the wind direction. As the surface water moves away from shore, the upwelling cold subsurface water takes its place. This results in water temperatures of from a typical 52 degrees in winter to 57 in mid summer. As Hedgpeth states in *Seashore Life,* "northern California has some of the coldest sea temperatures, for its latitude, on the globe."

This tends to discourage bathing along much of the region. The temperature range also discourages many of the life forms that like the warmer waters of southern California from venturing very far north. Even here, though, it is dangerous to generalize. In protected coves and bays, the water temperature in sections of the north are many degrees higher than the open sea. Thus members of more than one common southern California genus can be found in residence there. The question of how some of these inhabitants traversed the cold regions in-between is something else. However, from time to time there are unexpected water fluctuations that bring warm currents further north than usual or cold currents further south. Conceivably this is the reason for "cross-pollination" of some seemingly less hardy breeds.

In the uppermost shore zone, or spray zone,

Near the California-Oregon state line, the coastal redwoods give way to long stretches of smooth, sandy beaches bordered by seastacks.

the effect of the temperature is not as great and the life forms are identical, or at most only a little different, from those further south. Small white and brown barnacles are found on rocky areas of this kind. So is the usual assortment of periwinkles. Scurrying around along many of the rock faces are one-inch-long rock lice. A slender rock-colored mottled type called *Ligia occidentalis* is common from Marin County southward. To the north, though, another relative, *Ligia pallasi,* broader, longer and more uniformly colored, is the dominant species. In beach zones, the beach hopper and the beach flea are the major residents.

In the high intertidal, the constant color of the ocean floor is broken by patterns of plant life of various shapes and colors. Along protected coasts, snails and crabs wander among forests of waving olive-green or brown rockweeds. Their movements take them past fluted shells of such members of the limpet family as the brown and white shield limpet and *Acemaeus digitalis.* The latter, with its dingy dark brown shell, is the most common type from Monterey to Crescent City. And when its silver-dollar-sized body is cooked, it provides delicious eating.

Among the crabs that scuttle on top or hide beneath the rocks are the rock crab with its dark red or green square shell, the porcelain crab, and the crab often called the comedian of the intertidal zone, the familiar hermit. The hermit family is a large one, consisting of many members that vary in size, shell coloration, etc. The most common hermit in these waters is *Pagurus samuelis.* This crab, which often takes the shells of various large snails for its home, has bright red antennae tipping its olive drab, black-spotted body and often has bright blue stripes around the tips of its feet.

Some of these animals stray down to the middle intertidal zone, but the main members of this community are of different varieties. In the middle intertidal zone, the rock surfaces are often covered with herds of the aggregated anemone. When the tide is in, these animals look like patches of undersea foliage, seemingly rooted in place while their many tentacles wave in the drifting flow. They get their name from their appearance when the tide is out. Then they look like parts of the rock surface because of the many bits of gravel, broken shell, and other debris held on the tentacle surfaces.

Moving between rock barriers or beneath rock formations are other crabs, such as the purple shore crab or the straw colored hermit type, *Pagurus hemphilli.* Often found feeding on almost any kind of available animal life from sand dollars to barnacles is the six-rayed seastar *Leptasterias pusilla* or its relative, the Ochre star. Among the stalks and thin blades of the feather-boa kelp, one of the rare coral forms of the Pacific, the orange-red solitary coral *Balanophyllia elegans* can be found extending their polyp-shaped extensions from the cup-shaped shell base. This animal is related to the coral forms of the Pacific Islands and Florida, but it can't build up coral reefs or beaches under the cold temperatures and driving wave action of the Pacific.

Worms of many dimensions cling to rocks or make deep chambers beneath the sand or mud of the tide-washed shore. Typical are the scale worms, which look much like caterpillers, the sipunculid or "peanut" worms, and the tube worms that sometimes set up their series of cylindrical dwellings next to each other like a huge underwater honeycomb. Some of the ribbon worms found in protected zones on the underside of rocks are among the most brilliantly colored in the intertidal kingdom. These include the *Micrura veroilli,* whose slender body is striped with alternating lavender and white bands, and the *Paranemertes peregrina,* with white underbody and brown or purple surface.

Other denizens of this region are the various kinds of brittle stars—stars with tiny bodies and long, thin, wavy arms.

Where the waters of this zone are captured in shallow pools when the tide is out, a shore observer can sometimes catch sight of the transparent shrimp, *Spirontocaris picta.* The soft inner body of this energetic animal can be seen through its pale green shell, a shell sometimes made even prettier by a series of thin red stripes.

Most of the life forms of the protected coast cannot live in the exposed regions where the breakers shatter the rocks and beaches with thunderous force. But many a hardy animal or plant manages to exist under these circumstances. These include the California mussel and the goose barnacle. Untold thousands of both of these creatures can be seen in many of the remote coasts of northern California. Unfortunately, though the California mussel can take the direct shafts of ocean impact, it has been less fortunate with man. Many of this animal, which can be very tasty indeed in season (in summer months, though, it collects certain organisms which generate a deadly poison) were plucked from the ocean over the years. Many more, however, succumbed to the pollution of shore waters from sewage and other wastes in the vicinity of populated areas.

The low intertidal rocks are the home of some of the most famous species along California shores. These include many spectacular kinds of un-shelled snails, called nudibranches, which can be found in almost every color of the rainbow. Some of them are pulpy and shapeless, but others have long fingers extending from their bodies which can make them look almost like small sea flowers. An example is *Hermissenda crassicornis.* Its body is made up of many brown extensions with yellow tips that contrast with a white, triangle-shaped forepart creased by a slim needle-like appendage of bright yellow.

Also present in great numbers are the hydroids, which send their thin, many-branched extensions upward toward the light, exposing small brightly-colored leaf or flowerlike attachments. These creatures, such as the pink, fuzzy *Hydractinia milleri* or the ostrich plume hydroid, are dazzling to the viewer, who usually thinks they are a brilliant form of underwater bush. Actually, like the anemones, these are living, breathing animals.

There are also more kinds of crabs, snails, worms and limpets living here. Among the crabs of this zone are the deep red-colored *Cancer productus* and the olive-green kelp crab. Snails with shells sculptured in the shape of long cones, turbans and conches feed on the anemones. One of these is a member of the *Thais,* or purple, family. The reason for the name is the belief that the famed purple dyes used to decorate the togas of Roman officials 2000 years ago came from snails of this species.

Many of the large edible clams live where the low intertidal zone occurs in sandy mud. Among the most desirable are the Gaper clam and one that resembles it but usually grows to much larger size, the Goeduck. The burrows of the jackknife clam lay in regions enmeshed in the matted roots of stringy eel-grass.

The presence of eel-grass indicates a stage of the land's counterattack on the ocean's inroads. The eel-grass keeps the sand and mud in place, causing it to build up slowly until it is above the water line. Eventually, after a great many years, this section dries out and becomes an integral part of the land.

Chapter 4

The Great Northwest

THE STRETCH OF United States shore that is probably closest to its original, natural state can be found in Oregon and Washington. Only a few relatively small towns overlook its beaches and bays. The large cities in this corner of the country are not on the ocean but inland, on the banks of a large river, such as the Columbia, or lining the shores of Puget Sound.

There's a good reason for this. The trend toward colder temperatures, damp overcast and fierce storms in winter make these regions much less attractive for both large resort towns and seaports than the gentler regions of central and southern California. The presence of large bodies of water that penetrate deep into the back country offered early settlers the chance to establish port cities in places far removed from the often hard coastal environment.

Despite the hazards of the unprotected coast, there still are many marine dwellers that have found little trouble adjusting to the situation. In addition, there are many protected sections of coast and, in fact, a greater number of sizeable bays and inlets than to the south.

In many places the intertidal zone extends several times further seaward than in California. This is due to the increase in tide action as you proceed further north. The rise and fall of the tides is several times as great in this region, exposing considerably greater area of sea floor than the average shore of California.

The beach areas of the Northwest seem far less hospitable to the average visitor than those to the south or along the middle Atlantic and Florida coasts. For one thing, the sand beaches are far darker in color, coming close to being jet black in some locations. Many of the Northwest shores have no sand at all, however. Rather, they consist of jumbled rocks and cobbles that extend steeply only a short distance from the land. One reason for the irregularity of the Northwest shore compared to the smooth sand appearance of many California beaches is the relationship of an emerging coastline to a submerging one.

Geologists know that the land and water world are always changing position relative to one another in order to maintain a balance of forces. That is, forces build up in some parts of the earth's crust that tend to shift one section of land either upward or downward. When this happens, the surrounding land structure must adjust to compensate for this move. This might be compared to the escape valve on a pressure cooker.

When the pressure inside builds up to a certain level, the valve opens, allowing steam to escape. If the valve does not open, the inside pressure would rip the lid loose and hurl it into the air. Obviously, such violent reactions do occur in nature—volcanic eruptions and explosions, such as those that occurred on Krakatoa, have destroyed entire islands. In general, however, the earth's crust can adjust to changing forces without shattering results.

Thus over thousands or even millions of years, some parts of the land slowly shift upward and, to balance this, other sections move in the opposite direction. (In some cases, the balance may be a side-to-side movement of the two sections.) In central California, studies show that the coast is slowly moving higher, taking part of the former ocean floor and converting it to land. In this case, since the ocean bottom is relatively smooth sand or mud, the result is a good-sized sand beach. In the Northwest, the opposite movement is taking place. The ocean is moving in to take over sections of land as the land submerges. This has been going on for many centuries. The result is a sea floor that takes the shape of drowned hills and valleys and a beach that often is the residue of rocky hillsides.

Of course, even as this goes on, beaches are forming. One reason is wave erosion or the movement of soil down the many rivers that slice through Oregon and Washington. Because these rivers flow through sparsely settled regions of farmland or woodland or come down from the mountain chains that run parallel to the shore and about 20 miles inland, there hasn't been the drive to set up concrete flood channels or take many of the other flood control steps of population-rich California. This makes for a plentiful supply of natural sand to cover over many of the rocky slopes. In many places, the result is a smooth, wide beach during spring, summer and fall. In the winter, though, the storm waves cut back the beach to almost zero, exposing the jagged rocks of the subsiding land.

More so than to the south, however, many of the Northwest beaches have been formed by wave action against the coast. Much of the river-carried sand tends to pile up around the mouths of estuaries or bays rather than spread down along the coast. In other sections, the waves have gradually eaten into the land and covered the exposed rocks and cobbles with a thin layer of sand. Beaches formed this way are called young beaches by geologists, indicating that the sea level change that caused them is of fairly recent origin. However, the term "young" in geologic terms can mean anything from a few thousand years to 100,000.

A young shoreline is one of the three major types of beaches. A spit or bay-mouth bar and a barrier island are the other two major kinds. The first of these is well demonstrated by some of the features of the Northwest coast to be discussed a little later in this chapter. The barrier island form is common to the Atlantic Coast and will be reviewed in chapters dealing with that region.

The beaches of this northwest region look considerably different from those of California or the Atlantic Coast. The latter are light-colored, ranging from dazzling white to rosy pink. They

Lack of beaches is a feature of a geologically young stretch of shore such as Oregon's Cape Kiwanda near the northern end of Tillamook Bay.

are formed from billions upon billions of very fine sand grains. But those along most of the northwest shore are dark and, when examined closely, made up of relatively coarse grains of sand. The difference is due to the source of the sand. The light grains result from the weathering of granitic rocks, but the dark ones come from massive inland basalt plateaus.

The fact that basalt is a very hard material leads to another variation. The light colored sand beaches are not very firm when dry and you can easily sink your foot into them up to the ankle. The dark sands, on the other hand, form a surface that is usually very flat and hard enough to allow an ordinary car to drive over it without sinking in. (The coral beaches of Florida, of course, which also are made of a hard material, are just as firmly packed.)

The first white man to view these beaches, and the forest-clad slopes of the rugged Klamath Mountains and Coast Range that tower above them may have been the Spanish seaman Bartolomé Ferrelo. His voyage in 1542 is supposedly the furthest northern penetration along the Pacific Coast of the century. However, it is possible that he may have swung further out to sea and not have passed close to shore. More generally credited with the first report of this region is Sir Francis Drake, who went approximately halfway along the present Oregon shoreline before turning due west. It was not until 1775 that the first European landed in the region. This pioneer was Bruno Heceta, who landed near Point Grenville, about 30 miles above Gray's Harbor on the present state of Washington, and claimed possession of the region for Spain. Soon after, English explorer Captain James Cook made a more detailed examination of the shore. This was intended to help Britain's plans to claim the region, based on the influx of British fur traders into the Northwest.

It was the presence of many fur-bearing animals in the thick forests covering the Coast Mountains that was the main lure for the first settlers of the region. Many of those fur seekers were financed by traders from the fledgling United States. That included the ship captained by American Robert Gray that sailed along the Northwest shore in 1792. In the year that George Washington completed his first term as President of the new nation, Gray found the mouth of the mighty Columbia River and named it after his ship. Gray's discovery bolstered the United States claim to all the territory drained by the fresh waters of the river that today forms more than two-thirds of the boundary between Oregon and Washington.

It was not surprising that the mouth of even as mighty a river as the Columbia was not easily detected by dozens of experienced seafarers before Gray. The cold waters of the shore currents in combination with the massive barriers of the coast mountains result in climate that is very wet and overcast. The clouds moving eastward from the Pacific are quite thick in these latitudes and they pile up in front of the mountains until they give up much of their moisture in the form of rain or low lying fog. In addition, the rainfall along the Northwest coast is about 75 inches on the average, almost twice that of the

New York area and about five times as much as in southern California.

On a clear day, however, the dark beaches that stretch from Cape Ferrelo just above the California border, past the mouth of the Rogue River to Cape Blanco, and north to Coos Bay, serve to set off the spectacular scene of lofty snow-topped peaks of the Klamath Mountains. The large estuary that is Coos Bay has about as much shoreline as San Francisco Bay. But while the latter is hemmed in by buildings and factories, Coos Bay is only sparsely settled. Its blue waters gently lap 50 miles of tidal shore lined with green trees and dotted in summer with wild flowers.

Unlike the coast of most United States seaboard states, the shore of Oregon is fairly regular. Coos Bay is one of the few major inland extensions of the sea. As a result, the tidal shore of the state is less than twice that of the general coastline, which measures roughly 296 miles from the California border to the mouth of the Columbia River.

In the places on the outer part of Coos Bay that face the ocean, large sand dunes top a fairly steep slope that plunges down toward the shoreline. In winter, storm waves at the shore level occasionally reach the base of the slope and cut into the semi-permanent dunes, taking some of this soil out to sea. The surf zone slope of the beach is intermediate, dropping about 20 feet over a horizontal distance of about 800 feet. About 500 to 600 feet beyond the shoreline, this region is marked by a large sand bar that gives some protection to the coast on either side of the bay mouth.

This isn't the Sahara, but an unusual feature of the Oregon coast. Many of these sand dune formations are just a short distance from the ocean, in Jessie M. Honeyman Memorial State Park.

Giving up energy collected during a trip of thousands of miles across the open Pacific, waves pound against Seal Rock near Newport, Oregon.

Beyond Coos Bay, the shoreline recedes in an almost straight line at a shallow angle of about ten degrees. The coast is dotted with the mouths of a number of small rivers that empty into the ocean after running down the pine-clad sides of the mountains of the Coast Range. In general, the beaches are the usual dark fine-grained sand or cobbles. There is no major indentation until you reach the entrance to Tillamook Bay, approximately 40 miles from the Oregon-Washington border.

Above Tillamook Bay, the shoreline becomes jagged and hilly. It curves out to the projection of Tillamook Head, then swings in an arc another 15 miles north. Here the mouth of the Columbia, framed on one side by Hammond Point in Oregon and on the other by the sharp point of Cape Disappointment, comes into view. It was in this region in 1805 that Captain Meriwether Lewis and William Clark paddled their long war canoes to catch their first glimpse of the Pacific. The odds are that they saw little of Cape Disappointment, for it holds the somewhat dubious claim to fame of being the foggiest spot in the United States. For over 250 days a year, heavy gray clouds blanket the cape and its surrounding waters.

Lewis and Clark reached the Pacific in late fall and, having reached their goal, retreated a few miles from the ocean and crossed the sands of the Columbia River on its southern side to camp for the winter. They and their Indian guides chopped some of the plentiful trees to build Fort Clatsop within sight of the river bank. It was perhaps prophetic, for logging became the number one industry of the Northwest Territory and still holds first rank today. Some five years after Lewis and Clark spent the winter, the first permanent settlement was founded not far from the site of Fort Clatsop by members of the fur company owned by John Jacob Astor.

Some of the first residents of Astoria may have noted the broad stretches of sand that flanked both sides of the Columbia River mouth. Had they explored further up the coast into what is now Washington, they might have noticed a similar feature marking off the entrances first to Willipa Bay and then Gray's Harbor (also first discovered by the Captain Gray who baptized the Columbia River). If they did, they probably gave little thought to why these beaches were shaped and placed as they were. In recent times, though, ocean scientists who study this phenomena know full well that these three are excellent representatives of the type of beach called a spit or bay-mouth bar. They were formed by a combination of shore processes. Originally, the headlands around the mouths of the three waterways extended to sea in a sawtooth pattern. But the massive assault of Pacific storm waves ate into the headlands, changing their shape and ultimately forming the beaches around them because of a condition called wave refraction.

The causes of wave refraction were determined by oceanographers and hydrodynamicists, who examine the way fluids interact with solid boundaries. They discovered that initially, the wave energy in a wave front approaching land is equal everywhere as long as no subsurface obstruction is met. When the waves come close to land, their natural tendency is to take a position at right angles to the shore. But where there are headlands projecting into the ocean, the result is an arrangement that moves the waves toward the headland from all sides. As they get closer to shore the waves immediately around the headland are squeezed together while those that go past into the bay are spread apart. Because the enormous energy of the waves is focused on a small area, the result is a battering ram effect that eats into the land much more rapidly than on a straight shore. The erosion tears away particles of headland, taking them into the harbor to form a rapidly expanding beach.

The process continues until the headlands have been blunted. When this occurs, there is no longer a roadblock to the normal progress of longshore currents. Previously, the headlands prevented these currents from moving along parallel to the shore. Now, the longshore currents take the new sand eroded from the headlands and deposits it in a straight, continuous pattern parallel to shore. The eventual result is a series of long spits that block the wave's entrance to the waterway, thus turning it into a shallow, protected body of water.

In the case of the Columbia River, some of this action has taken place. However, a great deal of the sand that forms the huge spits on either side of the river mouth was collected from the steady stream of material carried seaward by the waterway. Once the sand from the Columbia reaches the ocean, the interaction of the river waters

Pine trees stretch down the slopes of the
Olympic Mountains almost to the
ocean on Washington's Olympic Peninsula.

Small cove beaches carved from rocky headlands by the
waves dot Oregon's northern
coast. Shown here is a beach near Cape Meares.

with the incoming current causes the sand to be distributed both to the north and the south. Some of the river-borne sand finds its way to the beaches that ring both Willapa and Gray's Harbors, too.

The northern end of the long spit at the mouth of the Columbia is called Ledbetter Point. This point forms the lower pincer (the upper is Cape Shoalwater) that threatens to turn Willapa Bay into a large inland lake. It also marks one of the most interesting locales for the study of multiple underwater sand bars. Profiles taken of the ocean floor off Ledbetter Point show it to have a very gentle slope characteristic of what oceanographers call a flat beach. (In 1,000 feet of distance from the shoreline, the water depth only goes down to 8 to 10 feet.) But the profile also shows the ocean bottom here to have three bars within approximately a half mile from shore. Though there are irregularities, depressions, channels, etc., and though the bars are changed by the currents, at least one of these stretches for 20 miles without a break.

Above Point Brown at the northern entrance to Gray's Harbor, the Washington coast veers westward toward Cape Flattery, unbroken by major bays or estuaries. For about half this distance, the coast is primarily gentle, sloping and covered with thick pine forests that reach almost to the water's edge. Then the scenery behind the beaches becomes rugged once more, signaling the beginning of the Olympic Mountains that cover most of the sharp northward pointing V that is the northwest tip of Washington.

The Olympic National Park ocean strip fronts

some of the wildest country left in the United States. The jagged tree-covered lower mountain slopes give way to soaring treeless snow-covered peaks. The peaks, which can be seen from the Pacific on one side and the waters of the Straits of Juan de Fuca on the other, include a number which have never been explored to date. The snow coverings are constantly replenished by one of the highest rainfall rates in the country— an average of 140 inches a year, which is three times the average rainfall of the American Northeast.

The Pacific Ocean shore of Washington measures roughly 157 miles in length. But the actual total coastline is over six times that figure. A glance at the map shows the far corner of Washington to be gouged out by a pie-slice-shaped boundary formed by the three straits that separate the mainland from Canada's Vancouver Island. The three straits are called Juan de Fuca, Huso and Georgia. Knifing deeply inland to the south is an extension of these waters called Puget Sound. As it winds its way through hundreds of islands, Puget Sound reaches into the Washington heartland a distance halfway back to the Oregon border.

When these inland waters are totaled up, the coastline of Washington expands to 908 miles. This figure does not include the shores of the aforementioned islands. Taking these into account would increase it to something over 3,000 miles.

The great expanse of shoreline in the protected areas from the Strait of Juan de Fuca to the bottom of Puget Sound provides abundant living areas for all kinds of intertidal life. Some of these are peculiar to the calm conditions of these inland shores where tides are so slight that the surf is practically non-existent. But a great many of the tidal residents of the region are found in abundance along the tide-lashed outer coasts as well.

The lure of Puget Sound for plants and animals might be compared to the attractions of its relatively mild climate for man. But despite the growth of large and bustling cities along the sound, including Olympia, Tacoma and Seattle, a great deal of this shore is still relatively untouched by industrialization and tract homes. That is why, for a time at least, Puget Sound remains one of the finest places for observing much of the types of life between the tides of the Northwest and, indeed, of the entire Pacific coast.

Unlike the sound, to which we shall return momentarily, the outer coast of Oregon and Washington is sometimes far from peaceful. In some places, where the land is submerging and the ocean waves' impact is consistent and thunderous, the large cobbled beaches are almost devoid of life. Luckily, the greater portion of the outer coast is protected by bars or has sufficient sand and mud to provide habitation for plants and animals. A good many of these residents— limpets, crabs, periwinkles and the like—are common to the coast from Puget Sound to Baja California, and have already been noted in previous chapters.

Some of these found in the high intertidal zones of the protected coast as well as the entire

Rugged stone cobble beaches like this are a feature of the Northwest coast of the United States.

coastline are the black turban snail, square-shelled red or green rock crabs and the isopods or pill bugs, which get their name from their tendency to roll up into tight little balls when threatened. In bays and estuaries of the Northwest, though, a purely local resident is the wedge-shaped mussel *Mytilus edulis,* which forms massive beds in some portions of Puget Sound.

The middle intertidal is thronged with thousands of different species. A small lined chiton called *Tonicella lineata* is considered one of the handsomest of the family to be found on the coast because of its unique shell decoration—sinuous lengthwise markings crossed by a series of horizontal lines that look like waves. The purple shore crabs scramble through the rockweed and under the rocks from the protected outer coast to the peaceful bays and estuaries. Also plentiful are brittle stars, several varieties of the primitive sponge family and, in protected tide pools, a black eel-like fish called a blenny.

In the open coast middle intertidal zone, the familiar California mussel and goose barnacle thrive. In addition, there is a species native to the Northwest called the Washington clam. The name Washington clam is given to a number of different clams, some of which are as native to southern shores as to the northern. However, the one designated *Saxidomus giganteus,* which has an average shell length of three inches, is usually not found below Puget Sound or in the quieter stretches of water along the northwest outer coast.

The low intertidal zone is frequented by many larger sized crabs, brittle stars and snails. Attached to the top armor of one of these crabs, the *Mimulus foliatus,* small colonies of vari-colored sponges may often be found. A large-clawed crab, the *Oedignathus inermis,* that resembles the fiddler variety, is common on the Oregon coast. In their wanderings these crustaceans sometimes go by the hiding places of the northwest octupus, the *Octupus dofleini.* This mild-mannered animal tucks its long suction-cup-lined arms close to its body and changes its color with ease to match its surroundings.

The rock oyster *Himnites giganteus* also blends in with the rocks in this zone. This oyster grows to six inches and more and is a delight to the palate. Thus it is eagerly sought by many skin divers in northwest waters. But this interest may soon wipe out the species, for the rock oyster requires 25 years to reach full size and most are now removed before reaching maturity.

As in all the life-supporting tide zones, the list of plant and animal population could go on for many pages. We might note, in passing, however, a few more of the striking creatures along the Washington and Oregon coast before looking briefly at the residents of Puget Sound. These include the white sea cucumber, which is found not only here but throughout the sound, the shrublike colonies of the tubeworm *Eudistylia vancouveri* and, in low intertidal tide pools, the large white shrimp *Spirontocaris brevirostris.* In many of the sandy bottomed tide pools the Cancer magister crab is found. Otherwise

Visitors often search for Washington clams in the tide zone of Northwest beaches.

known as the Dungeness crab, it is one of the most popular food items on Pacific coast restaurant menus.

Many knowledgeable visitors to the beaches of the Northwest can be seen slowly moving along the dark sands, heads down and with small shovels and buckets in their hands. They are watching for the signs of a burrow of the large razor clam, which has long been one of the major commercial seafood products of the region. However, with tourists digging up razor clams at a rate several times that of the commercial canneries, they may soon be only a memory, as is the case with several other forms of local sea life.

If the thoughts of rock oysters or razor clams found along the outer coastline make your mouth water, it is just an appetizer compared to the offerings of Puget Sound. Lodged in many limestone or hard rock homes in the sound are members of the edible and tasty rock-boring clam family. To harbor engineers, though, they are often a nuisance; these clams can drill their way into concrete and riddle a seemingly massive structure with thousands of holes. Another clam lives on many level gravel beaches in the quieter reaches of the sound. This is the rock cockle, also known as the little neck clam. This creature lives fairly close to the surface and its chalk white shell indented with a series of radiating ridges make it an easy mark for someone who wants a scoopful of the mollusks for a stew or chowder.

Rich groupings of oysters are also found in the sound, some growing naturally and some carefully laid out by oyster farmers. The Olympia oyster, the small white shelled *Ostrea lurida,* covers many rock outcroppings. It takes its name from the city of Olympia, which rises serenely along one of the lower shores of Puget Sound, and can claim to be the oyster capital of the Pacific. In the waters near the city, commercial oystermen tend large beds of imported oysters, mainly the *Crassostrea virginica* from the Atlantic Coast and the Japanese oyster *Crassostrea gigas.*

Puget Sound is also famous for its scallops with their beautiful fluted shells. The scallop is excellent eating and also provides the emblem for many sea motifs, including the shell symbol of the oil firm. And two of the distinctive crab residents of the sound are the Oregon crab, *Cancer oregonensis,* and the *Lophopanopeus bellus,* a crab notable for the deep black color of its claws.

Besides these species, the waters of Puget Sound teem with representatives of almost every shore family of the Pacific coast. There are anemones and limpets, chitons and snails, pill bugs and seastars, green urchins and bright red tunicates, to name a few. It is one of the Pacific coast's great natural treasure troves. Hopefully it will never, in time, go the way of the now almost sterile shores of San Francisco Bay.

Chapter 5

The Rockbound Shore

IT SEEMS APPROPRIATE that when the Pilgrims stepped ashore in New England in 1620, they landed on Plymouth Rock rather than on one of the sandy beaches that border a good part of nearby Cape Cod Bay. There are many miles of beaches dotting the sea periphery of the New England states, but the geologic features that set this area apart from the rest of the Atlantic Coast are rocks of all shapes and sizes.

Hard, enduring rock is the symbol of the area, a characteristic of the land as a whole. It also symbolizes the character of the settlers who overcame the hardships of long, chilling winters and thin, rock-filled soil to make New England the commercial heartland of early America. A good part of the region is hilly and mountainous, even though the highest peaks of the uplands are only a third as high as those of the Rockies or

Sierra Nevadas. Even where the land seems smooth and rolling, it usually takes only a little digging to uncover the surfaces of hard granite boulders.

Most of the beaches reflect the nature of the hinterland. Under a microscope, the tiny grains of sand are seen to be the minute fragments of granite or other hard volcanic rock. Much of this sand has travelled a long distance to get there, beginning in mountains and ridges that once soared skyward in the far north of Canada.

The story the rocks and sands tell has been deciphered for many years now by men of science. The boulder-strewn surface, the abrupt rocky coastline and the granitic sands stand as mute witnesses to the last stages of the Ice Age. In fairly recent geologic times, between 115,000 to 175,000 years ago, the earth's climatic conditions caused the polar caps to grow, thereby freezing more and more of the world's ocean. The frozen water became huge rivers of ice that flowed at snaillike speeds across the continents and weighed down on the land below with crushing force.

As these frozen rivers, or glaciers, travelled their path to the sea, they wore away most of the soil and split apart mountain ramparts into countless large and small boulders. For thousands of years, the moving ice mass carried the fragments of these mountains southward. When the Ice Age ended with the gradual thaw of much of the ice crystals, these rocks were left to mark the paths the glaciers took.

The great forces of the ice mass changed the face of the land in many ways. Huge holes were

Knifing its way between rock walls, the Atlantic sends a slender finger inland at Rafe's Chasm, Magnolia, Massachusetts.

gouged in the surface that became large inland lakes. The trees, vegetation and most of the soil of the previous age were wiped from the face of the earth. In fact, the entire shore of New England was drastically changed because of the tremendous pressure the ice mass exerted on the area for centuries. The weight of it literally ground the land down into the earth's crust. Then when the frozen water eventually thawed, causing the level of the seas to get higher, the ocean rushed in to flood the depressed lowland and make it part of the sea floor.

When Captain John Smith sailed along this coast in 1614 and named the region New England, he had no way of knowing how correct his use of the adjective "new" was. The drowning of the region's coastal lowlands occurred, geologists say, only about 10,000 years before, a time period as brief as the blinking of an eye in the age of the universe. Before this time, the New England shore extended far to the east, and a long strip of rolling wooded country separated the mountainous uplands from the shore. In those days, the shore was made of wide, quartz-filled beaches that had been formed at the same time those of the middle Atlantic and southern shores came into being. Today those ancient beaches lie hundreds of feet below the waters of the Atlantic.

The Atlantic has therefore moved up to the base of what were once inland hills, and the dividing line between land and ocean is a sharp rocky one. Because this event is so recent in geologic time, the forces of erosion have not yet worked their way on the shore. Eventually, in millions of years, barring some other change in conditions, the rock will be worn away and the sand particles, joined by others brought to the sea by rivers and streams, will form new wide beach strips.

Although we do not have to think about this eventuality now (we will continue to see the grass and forest in New England right at the water's edge in most places) some erosion of exposed land extensions has taken place in the last few hundred years and is already noticeable. An example is the tip of Long Island, a point of land that juts out eastward from the entrance to New York Harbor for some 150 miles. The site for Montauk Point lighthouse was reportedly selected originally by George Washington, who began his working career, history tells us, as a land surveyor. After studying the erosion rate, he decided that the beacon should be placed 200 feet in from the sea cliff at land's end. This, he calculated, would provide a life of 200 years. In 1960, about 170 years later, only 40 feet of land separated the edge of the sea from the lighthouse.

The areas of New England that were depressed and flattened by the glaciers apparently began near Long Island and encompassed the entire region to the north, including Nova Scotia and the Gaspe Peninsula in Canada. Thus the coastal plain that is now submerged extends from the tip of Cape Cod in an arc that swings past Nova Scotia and out beyond the easternmost shores of Newfoundland. A look at the map

The lighthouse at Maine's West Quoddy Head warns of the dangers of Maine's rugged shores.

shows that this drowned region is greater in area than all of New England and Nova Scotia combined.

The surface of the northernmost New England state, Maine, is pockmarked with lakes dug out by the glaciers. The steep rocky coastline of Maine is riddled with bays and inlets, too. Many of these inlets are narrow estuaries of rivers that cut into the Maine coast for 20 or 30 miles. A sampling of the estuaries of such rivers as the Narraguagus, Kennebec and Damariscotta show that the waters are mostly salty, thus part of the sea rather than the land.

These saltwater inlets resulted from the particular relationship Maine mountains and valleys have to the coastline. When the coastal plane sank beneath the ocean, the Atlantic waters rushed in to fill these valleys. The salt streams closed over forest and grassland and these stretches remain today as extensions of the mighty Atlantic.

All of this has resulted in the most irregular coastline in the United States. The direct length of Maine's coast is 225 miles, but total tidewashed shore comes to 3,478 miles. These shores include the tops of sunken hills, once actually part of the ancient lowlands, now surfacing as more than 400 offshore islands.

The start of Maine's "hundred-harbored" coast lies in the turbulent waters of Passamaquoddy Bay, which forms part of the boundary between that state and New Brunswick, Canada. The bouldered islands of Campobello (famous in the life of President Franklin D. Roosevelt) and Grand Manan monitor the flow of water in and

The tremendous swings of the Bay of Fundy tidal system is demonstrated in this pair of high and low tide pictures taken at Cutler, Maine.

out of Passamaquoddy—and it is one of the largest tidal swings in the world. In just one day, the difference between high and low tide can be as great as 15 to 20 feet.

The nearby Bay of Fundy is also part of the same tidal system. Just at the beginning of Fundy, the opening to Passamaquoddy appears. Whereas the latter extends to the north and forms part of the United States-Canadian boundary, Fundy runs eastward, at right angles to Passamaquoddy. The rolling waters of this bay move in a steep-sided channel between New Brunswick and the island of Nova Scotia, and the tides make those in Passamaquoddy seem tame. The dramatic movement of the sea along the 180-mile length of Fundy when the tide ebbs or flows is one of the most notable sights in nature. The change from high to low tide through most of the bay is 1½ to 2 times as great as in Passamaquoddy, but at the upper reaches, where the water is channeled into a narrow region called Chignecto Bay, the tides can vary the amazing amount of 50 feet.

The tides in this region provide the most striking demonstration of the nature of tides in general. As is the case for all tide action, the motivating forces are far removed from the surface of the earth. Tides are caused by the gravitational pull of the moon and the sun. The sun, of course, has far greater gravitational force than the tiny moon, but the strength of its pull is offset by its great distance from earth when compared to our natural satellite. Thus the most dramatic changes in tide flow can be related to the change in the phase and position of the moon. Nonetheless, the sun cannot be ignored, for without it, the tides would not act as they do.

In *Engineering Opportunities,* July, 1969, Dr. Irving Michelson, professor of aerospace engineering at Illinois Institute of Technology, defines the term tide as referring "to the regular and persistent rise and fall of the sea-level with periodicity of approximately 12 hours 25 minutes. Twice this interval, or 24 hours 50 minutes, is recognized as the average period between two successive risings of the moon. . . . A tide, in fact, means a rising and a falling of the ocean waters caused by the attractions of the sun and the moon."

When the moon and sun fall along the same straight line with the earth, an event that occurs at new moon or full moon, the gravitational pull of both bodies act together. When this occurs, the movement of the oceans is greatest, accounting for the highest ranges between high and low tide of the lunar cycle. These tides are called spring tides. If the moon's position to earth falls along a line at 90 degrees to the sun-earth line, the forces of gravity of the moon and sun are in maximum opposition. This results in the smallest tide variations, called the neap tides.

The animals and plants that live in the intertidal zones are marvelously attuned to these changes. Whether they live along the New England coast or the entire Atlantic and Pacific coasts, the creatures of the shores regulate their lives according to the rhythms of the solar system. A close look at the habits of these life forms throughout the lunar cycle shows that they adjust their patterns to meet the changes from spring tides to neap tides and back again.

The tides along most of Maine's coast, though, are far below those in Fundy. But in general, their range is somewhat higher than the worldwide average, which is 13 feet 9 inches for spring tides and 7 feet 9 inches for neap. It is interesting to note that despite the presence of Fundy and the higher tides in the New England area, the tide ranges along the entire Atlantic coast is far below the Pacific coast average. This is because the tides gain additional height and energy from the long voyage of the waves across the wide Pacific Ocean.

Just below Passamaquoddy Bay is the small city of Eastport, the easternmost city in the United States. Moving south-southwest along the coast, the shore is fairly straight until it reaches the indentation of Machias Bay. Here, from the pine-clad cliffs above the bay, hardy inhabitants might have watched as American sailors captured the British frigate *Margaretta* in the first sea engagement of the Revolutionary War.

Below Machias, the shore continues its sharp zig-zag course past Pleasant Bay and Frenchman's Bay to the rocky promontories of Acadia National Park. In Acadia, the waters of incoming tides batter a huge gap in the rocks with such resounding force that the spot is called Thunder Hole. At times, the onrushing waves hit the hole so fiercely that sprays of water are thrown 40 feet into the air. Here, too, rising sharply above the tide is the sheer face of Mt. Desert, whose rounded summit towers 1,527 feet above the sea surface. A short distance into Frenchman's Bay is the famous resort town of Bar Harbor, where brilliant green strands of pine trees come down to the water's edge.

The jumbled rocks continue to dominate the coastline, sometimes rising high in the air in sheer cliffs, other times forming low natural sea walls that front rolling meadows of trees and grass. Beaches are sparse in the eastern half of Maine, but there are small pocket beaches in many places. In addition, there is evidence that there is a slow rise of the land now that the glacial weight has been removed. This is proven by strips of beach now above high tide level that used to be submerged.

The ocean's largest penetration of the coast is found about 40 miles southwest of Acadia. This is deep and wide Penobscot Bay, located almost at the center of Maine's coast, 25 miles wide at its mouth and extending roughly 30 miles inland. Past Penobscot, the "fringed and tasseled" shore continues in a series of countless small bays and river mouths.

Near the small fishing town of Popham Beach, the combined waters of the region's major river system, the Androscoggin and Kennebec, meet the sea. These two rivers, the Androscoggin flowing down from the White Mountains of New Hampshire and the Kennebec from Maine's central highlands, join together at a location a few miles above the picturesque city of Bath, known for its typical New England shingle and clapboard houses. Below Bath, the combined flow takes the name of Lower Kennebec River. It was at the mouth of this stream that the first settlement in Maine, the Popham Colony, was founded by English colonists in 1607.

West of the Kennebec, the eastern third of Maine's coast takes on a different appearance. There are still many rocklined tide zones, but few of these stretches are high and precipitous. In many places, also, the rocks give way to long sandy beaches. The tides of broad Casco Bay just below Kennebec wash against many low grassy inlands and several wide marshy regions on the mainland. The shape of the bay provides many excellent, protected harbor fronts, a fact that led to the establishment of Maine's principal seaport and largest city, Portland, at its western end.

Past Casco Bay, the Maine shore is shaped like two connected shallow S's as it runs past many beach resorts and small fishing villages. Such names as Old Orchard Beach, Kennebunkport, Ogunquit and Kittery are famous to many eastern vacationers. From Kittery, an observer can look across the mouth of the Piscataqua River and see the docks of Portsmouth, New Hampshire's window on the world.

The ocean coastline of New Hampshire begins a few miles downriver from Portsmouth. This state has probably the shortest ocean coast of any in the union, measuring, in general, only 13 miles. Five broad, sandy beaches make up most of this shore. Adding to the tidal shore, though, are the islands of Star, White and Lunging, part of the Isles of Shoals which stretch roughly nine miles from the mainland. These islands help to boost New Hampshire's total tidal shoreline to 131 miles.

Like the lower half of the letter C, the coastline just past the New Hampshire-Massachusetts boundary curves down and up to Halibut Point on Cape Ann. Although it is part of the land mass depressed by the glaciers, this stretch of coast does not have the jagged indented appearance of the coast of Maine. The reason is topography. The raised portions of land run parallel to the ocean rather than at an angle. Also, the rocks here are almost solid granite, so the forces of erosion were unable to cut deep channels that would have provided gateways to interior valleys. Thus the sea could not pour past the rocky barriers and move far into the continent. This principle is seen along the shoreward rim of Cape Ann, where a guardian line of rock curves in a gentle arc above the line of beach below.

Around the corner from the cape, the coast juts sharply westward in an arc that forms the perimeter of Boston Bay, one of the most historic stretches of ocean in the country. In 1626, fragile boats from England landed the first settlers at a point near the northern edge of Boston Bay—a place the settlers named Salem. In 1629, they were joined by a religious group from England called Puritans. After a short time, most of the Puritans decided to found their own settlement and moved through the virgin forests to a well sheltered harbor on what is now called the Charles River. This was the Massachusetts Bay Colony, the origin of the city of Boston. Today, homes and commercial buildings line the shore of Boston Bay in a dense, almost unbroken concentration from Lynn on the north to the granite man-made canopy shielding ancient Plymouth Rock to the south.

Rounded hills that overlook many stretches of

beach or dock remind the onlooker of the grinding action of the ancient ice mass that once covered the state. Not the least of these is the Great Blue Hill that overlooks the Charles River and the southern part of Boston and is not too far from the Old North Church. It was from this church in 1776 that the sexton shone the famed signal lights that relayed Paul Revere's warning and told the townspeople whether the British troops were approaching by land or sea. The Great Blue Hill also provided the state name—Massachusetts translates from the Indian tongue as "the place of the great hill."

The shore between Boston and the Cape Cod Canal is low and sandy. The many shallow rivers feeding the region have brought great amounts of sand to the coast and the longshore currents have formed these into many long spits. For this reason the region is unsatisfactory, for the most part, for any maneuvering of large oceangoing vessels.

Sticking out from the lower coast of Massachusetts like a long J lying on its side is Cape Cod. The sandy beaches of the inside of the J form two-thirds of the perimeter of Cape Cod Bay. At the tip of the cape lies the harbor of Provincetown, where the Pilgrims first dropped anchor on the *Mayflower* after crossing the ocean from England. Here they drew up the famous plan for self-government, the Mayflower Compact, before leaving the inhospitable sand dunes of the cape to sail almost due west across the bay to Plymouth.

Though Cape Cod is only a small fraction of Massachusetts' land area, the combined sweep of

A section of Cape Cod's sweeping sand dunes.

A lone lighthouse stands a silent vigil
over the shore of Gay Head, Martha's Vineyard.

its inner and outer shores accounts for something like a quarter of the total coastline of 192 miles. The long slender cape contains broad beaches, often with dunes piled high a short distance inland, and with many low-lying swampy regions that are well adapted to the growth of cranberry bushes. The entire cape, plus part of the coast between the Cape Cod Canal and Plymouth, provide the bogs that make Massachusetts the largest supplier of the delicacy that goes naturally with the time honored Thanksgiving turkey. Roughly 60 percent of all cranberries marketed in the United States comes from the Bay State.

Though it juts into the ocean, only the bottom loop of Cape Cod's J is exposed to the full force of the Atlantic. The southern coast of the cape is protected by a narrow finger of land pointing southward called Monomy Island and the large offshore islands of Nantucket and Martha's Vineyard. These islands form the boundaries for Nantucket Sound, whose waters wash the beach of the summer resort of the Kennedy family at Hyannis.

A narrow string of islands, the Elizabeth Islands, stretches to the southwest from the lower western tip of the cape. On their southern side these islands form the boundary of Vineyard Sound that separates the mainland from Martha's Vineyard. The northern side of the Elizabeth Islands forms the lower boundary of Buzzard's Bay, whose waters flow against the remaining shore of Massachusetts from the Cape Cod Canal to the Rhode Island border. The offshore islands and the jagged indentations of Buzzard's Bay help swell the total tidal shoreline of the state to 1,519 miles. The city of New Bedford is located on Buzzard's Bay, and many a Yankee Clipper went forth from there in the 1800s to help build the nation's seafaring fame. Even now, whaling ships (now metal-hulled steamers rather than broad rigged sailing vessels) keep the city's fame as a whaling port alive.

About five miles beyond the Massachusetts border, the eastern half of Rhode Island's short (40 miles) general coastline is invaded by the sea. Just past Sakonnet Point, the wide mouth of the Sakonnet River flows into Rhode Island Sound, forming the eastern shoreline of Aquidnick Island. The southern shores of the island show the characteristic high rocky cliff formation of the region. Brenton Point, the westernmost spot on Aquidnick, looks across the entrance to Narragansett Bay to the western mainland of the state.

Flowing around many large and small islands, Narragansett penetrates northward for some 28 miles. At its lower end, its waves flow gently against the sheltered waterfront of Newport, a mecca for sailing enthusiasts and, until 1971, devotees of summertime jazz, folk and pop concerts. The beaches of many of the islands in Narragansett Bay are bordered by forbidding cliffs, but the mainland shoreline is generally made up of wide sand beaches and rolling grassy plains.

The western coast of Rhode Island begins at the town of Narragansett and continues for about 20 miles westward past the tip of Point Judith. The area that fronts the waters of Block

Rocky cliff formations typical of New England's young coastline can be found from Rhode Island to Maine. Shown here is part of Rhode Island's Mohegan Bluffs, rising 200 feet above the Atlantic and extending for five miles along the coast of Block Island.

Island Sound, which separates Block Island, 10 miles offshore, from the mainland, is low lying. Its sandy beaches and sand shoals are almost separated from the coast by shallow salt marshes and ponds. But beyond these sluggish waters and mud flats, the rim of rocky cliffs can be seen rising sharply a short distance inland.

West of Block Island Sound is Connecticut, the most westerly of the New England states. Fronting on Long Island Sound, Connecticut has the advantage of the protective barrier of Long Island between its shoreline and the Atlantic. The rock tiers of western Rhode Island continue part of the way from the border to the mouth of Connecticut's Thames River. At this point, though, most of the cliff formations have phased out. And newly outfitted atomic submarines cruising out to sea from New London naval shipyards pass broad white sand beaches where the Thames joins Long Island Sound.

The pattern of wide beaches, estuaries and small bays continues over most of Connecticut's 100-mile general coastline. The relative smoothness of the coast is indicated by a total tidal shore of only 612 miles.

Between the mouth of the Connecticut River that bisects the state and New Haven Bay lying about 30 miles to the west, the beaches become even more prominent. A prime example is Hammonasset Beach, approximately in the middle of this stretch, which extends five miles along the Long Island Sound. Further west along the Connecticut shore, from the mouth of the Housatonic to the New York border, smaller beaches and grassy areas that bring the color of bayberry and mountain laurel to the water's edge are found. In places along the length of the coast, too, the sea has moved beyond the beach barriers to claim some sections of land in the form of salt marshes.

The tidal life along the low-lying coastal regions of Connecticut are more closely related to that of New Jersey and the areas to the south than to the rocky open coast of most of New England. Relationship is uncomfortably close in another way, too: pollution from the residential and industrial towns concentrated between the port cities of Bridgeport and Greenwich flows steadily into the deceivingly calm waters of the sound.

From Cape Cod Bay to Passamaquoddy, the upper New England coast is under the domination of the Fundy tide system. Over most of this region, the spring tide range falls somewhere between 10 and 22 feet, depending on the form the sea bottom and land extensions take at any given location. (Cape Cod Bay has a range of 10 to 12 feet.) Nantucket Island just below Cape Cod, on the other hand, has the slight tide range of a foot. Why are Nantucket tides so small while Fundy's are 40 times as great? The answer illustrates the importance of shape. The wide mouth leading into Fundy and the high rocky sides of the nearby land compress incoming waves so that their energy is concentrated and their height is increased. The resulting inrush leaves an impact felt from Fundy to the cup of Cape Cod Bay. Nantucket, however, lies outside the Fundy tide system and is protected from the full force of the sea by Monomoy Island.

As might be expected, the great tide swings, coupled with the effects of the rocky coast, tend to reduce the number of tide life forms. The water from Cape Cod to Maine affects the situation, too. The water is cold because the warming effect of the Gulf Stream is withdrawn from the coast just about on a line with the cape. It is there that the Gulf Stream veers sharply out to sea, leaving the New England shore to the cold water from northern currents.

These conditions meet the need, though, of the New England lobster, found in great numbers in the middle and lower intertidal zones. This crustacean has made the region famous for seafood lovers throughout the world. The shadow of man has fallen over the species, however. The dumping of warm wastes from industrial and power plants into Maine rivers, for instance, warmed the offshore water in some areas so much that these places became unfit for lobster habitation.

Clinging to rocks in the upper tide zone or sandwiched into crevices are such shelled animals as the acorn barnacle and the rough periwinkle. The latter, a member of the snail family, has progressed from being an ocean dweller almost to being an air breather. After countless centuries, its gill cavity has developed the ability to extract life-giving oxygen from air when the tide has ebbed. This is in marked contrast to its relatives, the common periwinkle of the middle intertidal zone and the smooth periwinkle of the lower intertidal zone.

In the middle intertidal zone of the exposed coast, the large dog whelk in its easter-egg striped shell makes its way between forests of brown rockweed to feed on colonies of blue-shelled mussels. Clinging to many of the rocks are the shallow cones of the limpets, which eagerly devour the thin film of algae that covers many surfaces of sea girt boulders. When the tide ebbs, still other wonders are found in rock-rimmed tide pools. Here the fluttering movement of shrimp can sometimes be seen through the fronds of the red seaweed, called dulse, or the porous bulk of bright-hued sponges. Some of the many forms of worms or banded snails may also venture forth across the matlike growth of Irish moss that covers large tide pool areas.

The nereid worms and some of the other residents of the mid intertidal zone can also be found in the lower intertidal region. Here also are varied forms of plant life, including the oddly shaped sea potato and the brown *Laminarias.* The roots of these sea growths shelter colonies of many species, ranging from immobile ranks of mussels and deep-planted red-nosed clams to the highly mobile brittle stars. Another attractive resident is the golden star tunicate. Like the sea pansies of the southern shore, the tunicate is spangled with starlike gold clusters of separate little creatures which form an intricate colony around a green hub.

In the bays and coves of the New England coast, dense growths of seaweeds cling to rocks or sand bottom. These include the purplish-brown *Porphyra,* or purple laver, the orange-colored spiral wrack, and several other wracks of different hues. Between these plants, which rise to a height of many feet in the incoming tide, such species as the green crab, red shrimp and the plumed worm *Sprorbus* make their home. In many places, large colonies of eastern oysters also thrive, as do long-necked clams of several varieties.

The total number of species may be a bit smaller than other coasts, but the food potential of many of the New England tidal dwellers has long been high. The submergence of the original coast also provided excellent spawning grounds for fish in the raised portions of the drowned lands, now called offshore banks. These facts account for the many small fishing towns that dot the shores of the region and the picturesque sight of boats and nets vacationers have seen for many decades.

Chapter 6

Mid-Atlantic Coast

ALTHOUGH THE MIDDLE stretch of Atlantic coastline is the longest part of the eastern seaboard, it was not the first shore region to be observed and inspected by European explorers. Columbus landed on an island far from the North American mainland called Santo Domingo. Spanish, French and English navigators and captains probed bays and harbors in Florida, the Gulf coast and even along California before they paid much attention to the mid-Atlantic coast.

But this coastline still holds a special place in United States history, for it was here that the first permanent English colony was established at Jamestown, Virginia, on May 14, 1607, 13 years before the Pilgrims landed at Plymouth. The original settlers proved to be only the first of many waves of immigrants from the British Empire who crossed the rocky shores of New England and the wide beaches of the central coast to bring their language and traditions to this part of the New World. Jamestown in 1619 was also the site of the first elected governing body in the Western Hemisphere, the forerunner of the Virginia House of Burgesses of the following century. It was this institution (by then removed to Williamsburgh) that heard the footsteps and the resounding speeches of Patrick Henry and James Madison and that nurtured such quieter, but equally resolute men as Thomas Jefferson and George Washington.

The three ships of the expedition that founded Jamestown first made shore on Cape Henry. Captain Christopher Newport and his men landed briefly on this sandy headland before moving into the mouth of a large bay (now called Chesapeake Bay) and proceeding several miles up the body of water then called the James River. They went ashore to build their first shelters at a point approximately ten miles beyond the boundaries of the present city of Newport News.

The inland waters in those days flowed fresh and unpolluted to the Atlantic. A good share of edible fish of all kinds and a wide range of shellfish and other delicacies could be found there. Today, as in most parts of the United States, the waters carry chemical wastes, sewage and other substances that can upset the balance of nature for many river or ocean dwellers. Bustling docks and smokestack-turreted factories have replaced the ranks of trees and bushes that grew all the way to water's edge almost 400 years ago. Freighters and warships of all descriptions lie at anchor or steam slowly out of the roadstead where the three small sailing ships once made their lonely way.

But the rivers and the waters of the bay still carry their cargoes of sand from the mountains and fields of the American continent. These particles are still sorted and deposited on the wide beaches that front the mighty Atlantic. And the general system of beach formation that built the rampart of Cape Henry when the Indians were the only men roaming the eastern forests still goes on in the same way.

It is a cycle that has gone on for a long time. The central Atlantic coast is the oldest major population center in the United States and it is also one of the oldest in geological terms. Its age is demonstrated by the relative straightness of the shore from the mouth of the Hudson River all the way to the coral sands of Florida. There are many estuaries, bays and harbors inside this outer coast, but the sand beach itself curves around and down in a smooth regular line. A cross-section through the shore would show why this is so. The sea floor spreads toward the depths of the ocean in a long, gentle slope. Few submarine canyons break the surface of this Continental Shelf, which continues in most places for 100 miles before it ends in an abrupt descent to the true ocean floor, 10,000 to 15,000 feet below sea level.

This is a stable coast, too. That is, the entire region has moved very little over many thousands of years. This is in contrast to the West coast, for example, where sections of coast have been slowly submerging and other sections slowly rising.

Along the East coast from just below New York harbor all the way to Florida lies a string of long, narrow islands. These islands form the third major kind of beach mentioned in Chapter 4, the barrier beach. Ranging from one to three miles wide, these sandy beaches are separated from the mainland by bodies of water that vary in width from creek-size to over five miles. This long protected inner network of shallow bays provides a calm waterway in which boats can cruise almost the entire length of the East coast without ever having to venture into the rugged waters of the Atlantic Ocean.

The inland bays, though, are still connected to the ocean by means of inlets of various sizes that separate the long strip of sand into islands. These inlets may lie within a few miles of each other or be separated by barrier islands that run 20 or 30 miles long at a stretch. Thus the bays are subject to the ebb and flow of the tides. The direction of the tidal current, though, is often unpredictable because the flow through an inlet can be radically affected by the height of the ocean waves and the direction and intensity of the winds.

Oceanographer Fred Burrell illustrates this principle with a story about the man-made inlet that was cut between Manahawkin and Barnegat inlet on the barrier beach of the central New Jersey shore. The circulation pattern the new inlet set up with nearby Barnegat inlet can cause currents to surge through it at over 13 miles an hour. After sailing on one such current into the bay for the first time, Burrell calculated from tide charts when the current would probably flow the opposite way, and asked the tender of the drawbridge over the inlet if the bridge would be open then. The tender said he couldn't tell since it depended on the current direction. Hearing of Burrell's calculation, he chuckled, then said, "After 25 years I can't tell which way the current will go at any time. I only know that once it starts flowing in one direction, it keeps going that way for four to six hours."

The formation of barrier beaches is related to the presence of gently sloping shores that changed little over long periods of time. The sand carried into the oceans by rivers and streams was not obstructed by headlands, but was dropped a little at a time by the longshore currents in relatively straight lines. These deposits continued to build up, first in the form of underwater bars and later in the shape of protruding sand islands. This process has been aided by the winds that sometimes blow billions of grains of sand from the mainland out to the long, thin barrier beaches.

Although there are places today where the coast is open and exposed to the ocean's full forces, such as Long Branch, New Jersey, the barrier islands are, in effect, the Atlantic shore. And as such, it reflects the character of the land behind it. Rachel Carson, in *The Edge of the Sea* writes that "From Eastport to Key West, the sands of the American Atlantic coast, by their changing nature, reveal a varied origin . . .

"On Long Island, where much glacial material

has accumulated, the sands contain quantities of pink and red garnet and black tourmaline, along with many grains of magnetite. In New Jersey, where the coastal plain deposits of the south first appear, there is less magnetic material and less garnet. Smoky quartz predominates at Barnegat, glauconite at Monmouth Beach and heavy minerals at Cape May. Here and there beryl occurs where molten magma has brought up deeply buried material of the ancient earth to crystallize near the surface.

"North of Virginia, less than half of one percent of the sands are calcium carbonate; southward, about five percent. In North Carolina, the abundance of calcareous or shell sand suddenly increases, although quartz sand still forms the bulk of the beach materials. Between Cape Hatteras and Lookout in North Carolina, as much as ten percent of the sand is calcareous. And in North Carolina also there are odd accumulations of special materials, such as silicied wood—the same substance that is contained in the famous 'singing sands' of the island of Eigg in the Hebrides."

These shores are truly a world of sand. In the center of many of the barrier islands, the winds have piled the dunes up into miniature hills 20 or 30 feet in diameter, hills sometimes covered with a green facade of coarse grass or low shrubs. The main mass of these dunes remains in place year in and year out and is not constantly sieved and sorted by the waves and currents. In the same way, the mainland beaches, sheltered from the ocean's wrath by the barrier islands, are relatively stable, too, and a much more integral part of the coast than the shallow, shifting beaches of other parts of the American shore.

So stable are the center sections of some of these barrier islands that major cities of the Atlantic coast have been built on them. The most notable of these are Miami Beach and Atlantic City.

The most famous of all island settlements, however, New York's Manhattan, rises on solid rock and not hard-packed sand. Manhattan lies at the mouth of the Hudson River and is tucked well up into the upper of two large bays. The Upper Bay, whose waters wash Liberty Island, site of the Statue of Liberty, is pinched off at its lower end between the two boroughs of Staten Island and Brooklyn. This five-mile-wide strait, called The Narrows, leads to the larger Lower Bay that, in turn, feeds directly into the Atlantic.

We have noted that most of the beach along the central Atlantic shore is of the barrier kind. But the Lower Bay is framed by two long spits. To the north, Rockaway Spit was formed from sand carried to the sea by erosion of Long Island, the 150-mile wedge of land that is separated from the coast of Connecticut by Long Island Sound. The southern spit, a hook-shaped formation called, appropriately, Sandy Hook, grew from the erosion of the Navesink Highlands of the New Jersey shore. The tidal currents smooth and exchange sand between these spits and the long foot-shaped base of Long Island, the beach made famous in song and story for close to a century, Coney Island.

South from Sandy Hook, the shore is open to the ocean from Long Branch to Manasquan.

Little of nature's mark is left along the inner harbor shores of New York City, viewed looking north from the breakwater of Brooklyn's Erie Basin.

Then it takes on the typical coastal pattern and barrier islands front shallow, extended bays and mud flats. Most of the mainland coast of New Jersey is marshland, with narrow ribbons of water cutting between muddy sections of low-lying land topped by coarse grasses.

Below Manasquan, the barrier strip extends due south until Barnegat, while the coast curves away in a gentle westerly arc. After Barnegat, the barrier curves back at about a 45-degree angle, gradually narrowing the gap between the sand islands and the coast. Dozens of beach towns dot the islands—Seaside Park, Surf City, Beach Haven, Brigantine—but all are relatively small summer resorts until Atlantic City is reached just beyond Absecon Inlet. Strollers on the famous wide, wooden boardwalk of this all-year-round vacation spot look out on the ocean at a point approximately 60 miles from Cape May, which marks the end of the state's general coastline of 130 miles.

Once past the amusement parks and the massive resort hotels of Atlantic City, the long white beaches that stretch to the cape are only sparsely populated. Cape May forms the rounded end of a 30-mile-long finger of land that extends southwest from the lower New Jersey coast. The cape and its counterpart, triangular-shaped Cape Henlopen pointing north on the Delaware shore, mark off the limits of broad Delaware Bay. This bay is home to the waters of the mighty Delaware River, a waterway that begins in the Adirondack Mountains of New York. Once bright and clear, the river now is muddied with the sludge and sewage that is poured into it from the many major cities along its path—from Trenton and Camden in New Jersey, from Philadelphia, Pennsylvania, and from the city du Pont built, Delaware's major metropolis of Wilmington.

Although Delaware's tidal shoreline, which includes the marshy margins along Delaware Bay, totals 381 miles, the coast shore from the bay to the Maryland border measures only about 28 miles and consists of one single sand reef. The reef is penetrated at only one point, a narrow inlet found at its center. This connects the almost landlocked Rehoboth and Indian Bays with the ocean.

The entire state of Delaware is actually a part of a long hand-shaped stretch of land that includes the eastern third of Maryland and a thin sliver of land that is part of Virginia. This region, called the Delmarva Peninsula, lies between the Atlantic and a narrow 200-mile-long arm of the ocean called Chesapeake Bay. At the lower end of the peninsula a long pointing finger extends down to within 12 miles of Cape Henry, Virginia. This sliver of land accounts for about three-quarters of Virginia's total general shoreline of 112 miles.

Between the Delaware border and the base of Virginia's "finger," a small 31-mile stretch of Atlantic coast falls within Maryland's jurisdiction. This coast consists mainly of two long barrier islands, Assateague and Fenwick, that form the borders for Chincoteague Bay. As if to make up for the little of the Atlantic shore Maryland has for itself, the state dominates Chesapeake Bay. North from the mouth of the Potomac River,

Joining Virginia's eastern shore with the state's
mainland is the bridge-tunnel that spans the mouth
of broad Chesapeake Bay. The mainland of Virginia is
the far horizon with the Atlantic Ocean on the left.

Looking southward to Chesapeake Bay in the distance,
this aerial photo shows the Patapsco River
and most of the 45 miles of Baltimore's waterfront.

roughly 120 miles of the bay's length, the sandy beaches, chalk white cliffs and stretches of pine and fir trees fall within the boundaries of The Old Line State. As a result, Maryland's tidal shoreline is more than 3100 miles.

The lower Atlantic shoreline of Virginia extends only about 25 miles between Cape Henry and False Cape. Just below Cape Henry, though, it includes beautiful Virginia Beach. Beyond False Cape, in North Carolina, the barrier island chain bulges out to the east in a long sweeping curve that contains the promontory of Cape Hatteras at its furthest extension.

This is a region that has seen much in the way of landmark events of history. For example, the first heavier-than-air powered machine was flown by the Wright brothers on a desolate shore in this area. The site, Kitty Hawk, is a large windswept mass of duneland fronting Albermarle Sound at the start of the shore's arc. The date was December 17, 1903, and the fragile wood and fabric biplane rose barely high enough from its launch point on Kill Devil Hill for the pilot to catch a glimpse of the Atlantic swells just a few miles to the east. Today, a winged monument on the hill commemorates the event. But the 425-acre Wright Brothers National Memorial also serves to preserve the natural surroundings, an extra benefit to a nation that is rapidly altering most of its environment, partly due, ironically, to the fast-moving jet descendants of the Wright brothers' tiny vehicle.

The range of that plane, approximately 100 feet, was not sufficient to make the 10-mile trip to another renowned sand island to the south.

The second island, Roanoke, was the site of the first colony ever established by England in the New World in 1585. That colony did not last, however. It fell prey either to disease or Indians. The mystery of the disappearance of its population is as great today as it was in 1590, when the crew of a provision ship found no trace of the colonists other than the word "Croatoan" carved on a tree.

The curving barrier chain anchored by Cape Hatteras encloses the immense Pamlico Sound which separates the barrier islands from the mainland by some 25 to 30 miles of water. The islands in the area and the matching sweep of mainland in Dare County form the Cape Hatteras National Seashore. Here the interlocking network of sand, trees, scrub and small rivulets are hardly changed from the day in the year 1524 when the region received its first visit from a European explorer, the Florentine sea captain Giovanni da Verrazano. Many ducks and birds of brilliant hue make their homes in the swamps of the seashore and a considerable variety of intertidal life forms thrive in the confines of Pamlico Bay.

Included in the preserve is Cape Hatteras, known for its lighthouse that warns ships away from the submerged sand bars and scattered offshore reefs. The bars and the reefs, made from a soft claylike rock known as marl, have claimed many a ship over the years when roaring Atlantic storms or fearsome hurricanes moving north from the Caribbean have obscured the warning lights on the cape. More recently, a lightship has been permanently stationed some 13 miles out

Breaking the symmetry of green foliage, white beach and blue-green ocean is man's contribution, the Sea Pines golf course on South Carolina's Hilton Head Island.

to sea where the edge of the warm waters of the Gulf Stream skirt the Carolina shores.

The sweep of barrier islands comes back close to the mainland just above the town of Beaufort. Positioned above Beaufort is a thin barrier island tipped by Cape Lookout. Below Cape Lookout the confused mixture of sand, silt and churning tides causes a series of shoals, or shallow areas, with such names as Diamond Shoal, Frying Pan Shoal, Shark Shoal, Sheepshead Shoal and Bird Shoal. At low tide, many of the long ridges of sand bottom in these regions are covered only by a thin layer of seawater for miles around.

For several hundreds of miles below Beaufort, the shore is scalloped out by two long, shallow bays. The first of these is Onslow Bay and the second, which straddles the state line between North and South Carolina, is called Long Bay. The barrier islands fronting on the bays are separated from the mainland by such narrow streams, they almost seem connected to the coast. Long stretches of these shores are barely touched by civilization. If you wandered along the deserted white sand barrier beaches or worked your way through the tree and vine-covered marshland only a short way inland, you could imagine pirates of old searching for places to conceal buried treasure.

Such thoughts go well with the name of the point just beyond Carolina Beach where the scallop of Onslow ends and that of Long Bay begins. This is Cape Fear, a triangle of land jutting into the Atlantic. It gets its name from the fearsome rain and gale-wind storms that boil up on the ocean near here many times a year. As in the Cape Hatteras area, sunken reefs and bars await any ship that ventures too close to shore.

In the middle of the smooth curve of Long Bay, one of the best-known beaches of the region, South Carolina's Myrtle Beach, is found. Sunbathers lolling on the broad strand can gaze at reaches of green-blue ocean to the east or look westward to the bright blue-green leaves of a fragrant backdrop of myrtle bushes. At certain times of the year, the beach is bordered by patches of the flat white flowers of this evergreen.

The shore becomes increasingly spongy to the south. Wide stretches of salt marshes nurture the growth of vine entangled cypress, gum and bay trees. Scattered here and there on the tropic-like coastline are the sharp-spiked leaves of the palmetto. Past the mouth of the Santee, the shore becomes increasingly irregular. More and more islands, large and small, some sandy and some marshy, make a patchwork pattern between the Atlantic and the coast.

About 45 miles from the Santee, a series of small marshy islands ring the approaches to South Carolina's major seaport, Charleston. Midway between Sullivan Island and Morris Island, which form the gateway to the harbor, a squat, dark red-brown building sits on its own small island. This now lifeless mass of masonry is Fort Sumter, the focal point of the first blazing encounter of the bloody Civil War in April, 1861.

Between Charleston and the Georgia border, the shore continues to be increasingly fragmented by an ever-greater number of islands. Two large sounds, St. Helena and Port Royal, divide the region into three rough segments. The waters of the latter flow seaward past the low-lying shores of the most famous of all training centers of the U.S. Marines, Parris Island.

The Georgia shore only totals 100 miles in direct length from South Carolina to Florida. But the fringe of islands, and the succession of streams and rivers that carve much of the inner coast into sounds and bays, give it a total tidal shoreline of 2,344 miles. Behind the fringe of beach, much of the shore is colored a deep green by a dense undergrowth of tall grass, shrubs and palmettos that surrounds the ranks of overhanging trees. Just past the South Carolina border, the waters of the Savannah River twist and turn their final few miles to the sea, running past dozens of tree-lined islands and salt marshes. Just above this region, one of the most scenic along the coast, the port city of Savannah is slowly expanding north and east, bringing cries of alarm from conservationists as each island citadel is conquered by real estate subdivisions for new outposts of suburbia.

Below Savannah, the coast is fronted by a series of long narrow islands beginning with Ossabaw and proceeding through Blackbeard, Sapelo, St. Simons and Cumberland. Most of these are fringed with white quartz beaches. Sapelo and St. Simons, however, also have wide stretches of dark hued sands. These "black sands" are made mainly of rutile and ilmenite, substances of volcanic origin. Both of these minerals are of great value to man because they contain large amounts of the metals titanium and iron. Rutile is the source of a titanium compound called titanium oxide, a material that makes one of the best pigments for white paint. Ilmenite, on the other hand, is the prime source of the metal titanium, a material that can withstand the searing heat of flight at incredibly high speeds.

The color of the sand, of course, does not bother the sea animals that make their homes in the long tidal flats of the Atlantic coast. The horseshoe crab, the sea mouse, the burrowing clams and the lobsters of varied size and pigment make their homes indiscriminately along the shores of Sapelo and St. Simons and throughout most of the shore from Georgia right up to the tip of New England.

There are, of course, some differences from one region to another even though the families are widely represented. The middle intertidal starfish *Astropecten,* which burrows into the sand for protection and camouflage along the shore of New Jersey, Delaware, Maryland and Virginia, is five-rayed as is its cousin of the Carolinas and Georgia, *Luidea.* But its rays seem short and stubby while *Luidea's* are long and thin.

Along two regions of the tidal shore, the high beach and open ocean coast, the life forms are relatively few in number, as they were on the West coast. Where the Atlantic waves hit the exposed coast with punishing force, the main residents are some members of the crustacean phylum and one or two kinds of mollusks. The former cling to rocky outcropping or low reefs and include the gooseneck barnacle and the acorn variety. The mole crab, a creature that

Fringing many sections of the Atlantic shore along the Carolinas and the Georgia coasts are giant wild sea oats.

Angel wing, starfish and seahorse are just a few of the tidal residents of the Carolinas shown in this picture.

looks like a large relative of the ladybug, digs in beneath the surface when the waves rush in, then extends its two feathery appendages to search for food morsels when the backwash frees the shore from the sea's grasp for a moment. The small coquina clam of the mollusk class *Pelecypoda* disdains the security of a rock attachment and, with shell closed, takes the buffeting of the waves with seeming indifference. The coquinas' slender, multi-colored shells beautify many beach areas after the animal has died.

The high beaches are the habitat of our old friend the beach hopper, already noted as a common resident of Pacific beaches. Peculiar to the Atlantic, though, is the quartz-colored ghost crab, a creature that usually stays hidden in its sand burrow during the day and comes out to look for food after the sun goes down.

The low middle and low intertidal zones from New Jersey to Maryland are populated by the surf clam, with its heavy shell armor, and many of the large shelled whelks. These giants of the snail family make their way among the sea grass and bryozoans looking for their favorite food, clams. Sometimes, though, a stone crab, with its deep purple body, scuttles forth to crush the whelk between its massive pincers. Members of the oyster clan, including the blue points of Chesapeake Bay fame, settle in many protected sections.

Other members of the shellfish family make their appearance from Virginia to Florida. The Ponderous Ark, with its large ribbed shell, occupies crevasses in the intertidal world. So does its cousin, the turkey wing. The Pens, with their long, dunce-cap-shaped and delicately gold-colored coverings, are also found in great numbers.

In the middle intertidal, the dwellers along the entire coast include such varied forms as the blue crab, the eastern fiddler crab, the pentagonal sand dollar and, in rocky areas, date mussels, angel-wing clams and snails of many sizes and shapes. In many of the long, shallow, gently sloping tidelands, patches of sea pansies make their home. Shaped somewhat like a mushroom, each of these flowerlike systems is actually a colony of hundreds of tiny tubelike creatures that join together to extract their lifeblood from the sea.

Some of these creatures live as well in low intertidal, moving among the stems of the sea grasses and, in places, brown sargassum weed. Other life forms throng the deeper zone, though, including the calico crab, with its bright red spotted carapace or case, the sand anemone and many red, orange and yellow sponges.

Life on these shores goes on in many places just as it has for countless ages. In a number of areas, where sea gulls swoop across the white-capped waves, wild deer come down to gaze at the landscape and alligators ease their way between islets. This is particularly true for much of the southern coast. But the handwriting may be on the wall. The factory wastes, sewage and oil sludge finding its way to the oceans in the industrial north already have disturbed the balance of nature for shore life there. As man claims more of the shore for living space, a somber fate awaits many unsuspecting life forms along the lower Atlantic coast as well.

Chapter 7

The Gulf Coast

THE GULF OF MEXICO presses against the bottom of North America like a large balloon, as if it were trying to compress the western shores into a narrow land bridge separating North and South America. The stopper in the balloon is Cuba, lying midway between the two pointed fingers of Florida and Yucatan. On either side of Cuba, currents flow in and out of the Gulf through the Straits of Yucatan to the south and Florida to the north. These currents, part of the system that gives rise to the Gulf Stream that flows northward along the Atlantic coast, are relatively warm.

Although the Gulf of Mexico is part of the Atlantic Ocean, its waters are about seven degrees warmer. This is partly due to the warmth of the Gulf shores. The nearness of the region to the equator results in a climate that is tropical along much of the Mexican coast and near-tropical along the curving Gulf shore of the United States.

The temperate climate in Mexico probably had a lot to do with the growth of the great Indian civilizations in this region. It was the wealth and luxury of the Aztecs that helped lure the plunderers from Europe who started the exploration and colonization that eventually led to the conquest of the New World by immigrants from the old.

There was certainly a lot of shore to probe. The general extent of the entire Gulf coast from the tip of Florida to the tip of Yucatan measures more than 3,000 miles. The tidal shoreline, which includes all bays, inlets and estuaries, is considerably larger, totaling over 6,000 miles. The tidal shoreline of the United States Gulf coast from Brownsville, Texas, to Key West, Florida, is about 4,097 miles, making this coast the second longest, after the Atlantic region.

Even subtracting the Gulf coast region of Florida, which is considered in the next chapter, the region arbitrarily considered by most to be the Gulf coast is longer than the United States Pacific shore. From Brownsville to the Alabama-Florida border, the general shoreline is about 1,500 miles and the tidal shoreline approximately 3,000 miles.

Explorers from Latin lands were travelling the shallow, generally placid waters of the Gulf of Mexico for decades before the penetration of the Atlantic shores began. Amerigo Vespucci claimed to have travelled past the tree-clad banks of the Gulf coast in 1497, though historians are far from agreeing that he actually did so. But it is certain that Spanish adventurers set foot on the Gulf shore in what is now Alabama's small coastal panhandle a little over two decades later. A plaque placed in Fort Morgan, which once dominated the entrance to Mobile Bay, states, "In memory of Alonso Alvarez de Pineda who landed here in 1519, being 101 years before the Pilgrims landed at New Plymouth."

In later decades other explorers, French and Spanish, examined the long, curving shell beaches and the matted growth of water oaks and magnolias that came down to the water's edge in many places. The native countries of many of these adventurers, the sun-drenched shores of Spain and southern France, had similar climates. It might have been expected that once word of Gulf conditions reached home, hoards of colonists would set forth.

This was not the case, however. Perhaps the heavy, moisture-laden air, the masses of dead tree branches and driftwood that seemed to bar the entrance to many of the rivers, or the psychological effects of such shore creatures as alligators and huge snakes tempered any glowing reports. Too, the first explorers perhaps preferred to downgrade the colonial potential of the new lands as a method of keeping competition for the expected treasures of gold, silver and precious jewels to a minimum.

Whatever the reasons, the sandy islands, salt marshes and narrow lagoons of the area were trodden mostly by animals or Indians until long after colonies were established and thriving in New England and the mid-Atlantic regions.

The Spanish, of course, had colonies in Florida

during the 1500s, but it was the French who first settled in the humid regions of the mid-Gulf coast. Pierre Le Moyne, Sieur d'Iberville, led his band of French-Canadian settlers ashore through the tall pines and waving grasses on the Bay of Biloxi in 1699. The location of this first settlement was on the east bank of the bay, across the water from the present site of the city of Biloxi.

It only took a little while for the government of the French colonial region named Louisiana, after King Louis XIV, to decide that the threat of malaria and other sub-tropical illnesses made this site relatively undesirable for habitation. The brother of Iberville, Jean Baptiste Le Moyne, the Sieur de Bienville, was sent eastward, where he broached the narrow entrance between the wooded shores of the island he named Dauphin and the long narrow peninsula to the east (now called Mobile Point) and entered Mobile Bay. Once past the mile-wide gateway, he found himself on a broad inviting waterway some 10 miles wide at the base and stretching smoothly 30 miles to the north.

Bienville sailed up the bay, noting the high ridge on the east bank topped with countless pine trees (it still is), and the varied vegetation, including magnolias, azaleas and rolling grassland to the west. The settlers cruised the length of the bay and went 27 miles up the Mobile River where they founded the town of Mobile in 1702. In 1711, that first town was flooded and Mobile was moved to the head of Mobile Bay, where it has developed into the major industrial city it is today.

The eastern boundary of the Gulf coast lies

only a short distance from the entrance to Mobile Bay, where the Perdido River separates Alabama and Florida. At the base of the river, the narrow, 10-mile-long Perdido Bay, fringed with swamps and semi-tropical plants works its way to the Gulf between the Gulf Shores Peninsula of Alabama and one of the narrow coastal islands of Florida's panhandle. From Orange Beach to Mobile Point, Gulf Shores beaches stretch smooth and white for 30 miles. Healthy growths of oak and pine crowd down to the beach perimeter on a solid foundation of clay soil.

This stretch of beach accounts for most of Alabama's 53 miles of shoreline. The entire tidal shoreline, however, covers a total of 607 miles. At the tip of the Gulf Shores Peninsula, old Fort Morgan looks across the bay mouth to Fort Gaines and Dauphin Island. From these forts, Confederate batteries sought to prevent Union gunboats from entering Mobile Bay in the engagement in which Admiral David Farragut exclaimed, "Damn the torpedoes! Full speed ahead!"*

Dauphin is the easternmost of a series of long and narrow islands fronting the coast from Biloxi to Mobile Bay. Twenty miles of western Alabama coastal shore and 10 miles of the neighboring Mississippi panhandle consist of firm white sand beaches backed by green stretches of trees and shrubbery. In many places, the trees may be any of 20 different varieties of pecans that grow in a great part of the southeastern region.

*There is some question among historians as to whether Farragut said "Full speed ahead" or "Go ahead!"

Low-lying wooded islands rim a good part of the Gulf coast.

Near the city of Pascagoula, the scenery changes. In the waters of Mississippi Sound, barges tow strange man-made steel towers, hallmarks of the oil drilling rigs built for offshore fields in the coastal waters of nearby Louisiana and Texas. The landforms turn to low-lying marshland where the waters of the Pascagoula River enter the sound. But after some four to five miles of marshland on the west bank of the Pascagoula, the shore firms up once more and the evergreen of countless pine trees almost meet the quartz beaches that stretch for 20 miles to the Bay of Biloxi.

The bright blue water of the bay contrasts sharply with the muddier tone of the Gulf of Mexico, so darkened from centuries of silt carried south to it from the rivers of America's heartland. Biloxi, Mississippi's third largest city, is situated on the west bank of the bay. The masts of one of the largest shrimp fleets on the Gulf dot its waterfront, which extends three-quarters of the way around the peninsula-based city. Massive freighters, too, make their way past Cat Island to the bustling docks of this city.

Beyond Biloxi's western limits, a broad four-lane highway runs like an arrow behind an almost unbroken 27-mile stretch of white sand. The only interruptions are the waterfront areas of such towns as Gulfport and Pass Christian. For the most part, the highway is a sharp dividing line between gently sloping beach and a backdrop of green foliage and lawn.

The stretch of coast between Perdido Bay and the Pearl River, the boundary between Mississippi and Louisiana, is one of peaceful beauty.

Hodding Carter, in his book *Gulf Coast Country,* notes, "The sea, close to the coast, is mild, for it is fended by a low barrier of islands; and even the hurricanes that now and then howl in from the Florida Keys are less destructive, more sparing of life, when they approach here. . . .

"Behind the sea wall, broken by the hurricane of 1947, run the pine forests, the low savannahs, the white sand, and the abiding lagoons. Here on a long and narrow strip that extends so short a way inland lie the foliage-hidden homes of beauty and of squalor, blessed alike with the shade and the scent of flowering bushes and of a multitude of trees. The soughing pine forests and the moss-hung oaks come down to the sea itself, down from the sandy meadows and the inland hills of red and yellow clay, the rolling despoiled land of slow recovery. It is a lavish, untended beauty, direct from the womb of nature, and maltreated by man. Behind the one principal highway, little shell-white roads wander seemingly without purpose beneath the oaks and the mimosa and thick trailing vines in a helter-skelter disregard for civilization, as if the very land has caught the unregulated spirit of the people. Or perhaps the process was the other way around."

Beyond the Pearl River, the shore changes dramatically. The coast gives up its solidity and takes on the look of a water-logged bog. This is the start of a region where the land and the sea are intricately intertwined. It is a region completely dominated by the irresistible flow of the "father of waters," the mighty Mississippi River. Fed by hundreds of streams and rivers for its

Five tugboats at the top of the photo move a new oil-drilling rig down the Mississippi from New Orleans where it was built towards its location in the Gulf of Mexico.

1,000-mile length, the Mississippi ceaselessly brings its cargo of soil from Canada and several dozen states to build up the shore and the sea floor of the Gulf.

Twisting snakelike through the lower section of Louisiana, the Mississippi feeds countless offshoots of tiny streams, broad lakes and minor rivers that dot the brown-green land like shining mirrors when seen from the air. The river also supplies the lifeblood of water traffic for the queen city of the Gulf, fabled New Orleans, which is located on several of the broad sweeping turns of its muddy lower reaches. The location of the city accounts for its nickname of the Crescent City. When Sieur de Bienville founded it in 1717, he reported he established it on "one of the finest crescents of the river." The river in those days was called Fleuve Sainte-Louis, a title given it by the great French explorer La Salle, who claimed the entire region drained by the Mississippi for the King of France in 1682. When it became the new capital of Louisiana, Bienville was ordered to name the city Nouvelle-Orleans, in honor of Louis Philippe, duc d' Orleans, who was regent of France in 1717.

Bienville had to travel 110 miles up the low, marsh-surrounded, tree-lined banks of the Mississippi to found his new town. From centuries of depositing soil at its mouth, the Mississippi had built up a long slender neck of land that extended east-southeast into the Gulf, called the Mississippi Delta. In truth, the entire lower section of Louisiana was built up in this way. At one time, ages ago, the Mississippi reached the sea in a continuation of its almost due-south course through the middle of North America. As it built up the low-lying portions of the Gulf and these began to rise above sea level, the river was shunted more and more to the east. Now it travels almost directly east from Baton Rouge to New Orleans before breaking free of its self-imposed land barriers to reach the Gulf below New Orleans.

The fact that New Orleans and its surrounding regions were once part of the Atlantic is brought home by the nature of the shallow lakes that bound the city, Lake Pontchartrain and Lake Borgne. Both of these broad bodies of water are salty, not fresh, and Lake Borgne actually provides New Orleans with a direct opening to the Gulf by a channel at its eastern end that passes around Grand Island. Many of the cargoes to and from the upper Mississippi don't continue down the river past the gleaming towers of modern New Orleans or the quaint ironwork grilles of the old French parts of the city. Instead, they move by way of canals through Lake Borgne or down into Breton Sound in a ship channel that passes between Breton Island on the south and the lower end of the arc of Chandeleur Islands. The Chandeleurs form a protective rim against Gulf storms about 40 miles to the east of the fringed end of Orleans Parish.

The coast near the mouth of Lake Borgne is a network of small portions of soggy marshland separated by various sized channels of water. These sections, extending to the waters of Chandeleur and Breton Sound, look from the air like a mass of brown and green confetti thrown haphazardly into the sea by some huge hand. The wildly indented shore extends down and around the Mississippi Delta, then back to the northwest to the equally jagged shores of Barataria Bay. Barataria is the first of a series of saltwater bays pockmarking Louisiana's middle shores. After Barataria come Timbalier, Terrebonne, Caillou, Atchafalaya, Blanche and Vermilion. Hundreds of the famous bayous that are one of Louisiana's most prominent features drain into many of these bays.

To the average Louisianian, a bayou is considered to be just another word for a river. Strictly speaking, a bayou is a slow-moving inlet or outlet of a lake, bay or river delta. One of the largest of the bayous is the stream called the Atchafalaya River, whose waters reach Atchafalaya Bay by way of Lake Charenton. At one time in the distant past, the bed of the Atchafalaya was the main route of the Mississippi to the Gulf. It became a bayou after the rising level of the muddy bottom forced the river to cut a new course eastward. Even now, in times of flood, the Atchafalaya receives the overflow from the Mississippi through great man-made concrete spillways that drain off any water that pours over the tops of the vital levees.

Some readers may wonder why the action of the Mississippi built up the land so quickly when compared to the relatively slow changes caused by the rivers of the other coasts. There are many factors favoring Mississippi Delta growth. For one, the Gulf of Mexico is not subject to the great wave actions of the open ocean regions. Its slower movement tends to let particles reaching

This isn't a fishing flotilla, but a typical congregation of offshore oil rigs in one section of Texas coast. As the close-up of one of these towers indicates, these are massive metal structures housing many men and various equipment used in oil operations. Along the Gulf coast of Texas, Louisiana and Mississippi, oil rigs can be found close to shore or as far out as ten miles.

it settle close to the shore in great amounts. In addition, the Mississippi drains such a wide area that it has vastly greater amounts of soil in its flow than any other river in the United States. Finally, the Gulf itself is shallow, with depths of 10,000 to 12,000 feet occurring only in limited sections. Close to shore, the Gulf has a long, gentle sloping subsurface that is free of the huge submarine canyons that drain off silt and sand from the rivers of the Pacific coast.

The effect of all the many bays and other coastal inlets on the Louisiana coast is a tidal shoreline even greater than that of Florida or Maine. Coast Guard estimates indicate a total of 7,721 miles. Louisiana's general coastline length is only 397 miles, but this is not a small coast. This length is the fifth longest of all the states, exceeded only by those of Alaska, Florida, California and Hawaii.

Almost the entire Louisiana coast is marshland, but the most water-logged part of it is the stretch from the shores of Lake Borgne to Timbalier Bay, where the shore is a mixture of green marsh grass and water. Sometimes the grass seems to stretch for miles; other times it is pierced by wide, but shallow lakes or ponds. It is treacherous country, called the region of "trembling prairies." The "land" looks solid, yet is so watersoaked that it gives way easily to the foot. Where this region blends into the Gulf, there are long stretches of dark sand beaches (mostly littered with all kinds of junk ranging from beer cans to campfire remains). Increasingly, a manmade forest of oil derricks is lining up several miles offshore. Some of the richest deposits of this all-important fuel were found here in the years following World War II.

To the west, from Atchafalaya Bay to Vermilion Bay, the shore is swampy, but more solid. The slow-moving bayous and salt water inlets reflect images of wild tropical grandeur. Moss-hung live oaks, scrub banana plants, green bushes of every type and description hug the water's edge along many of these waterways.

Beyond Marsh Island, which lies between the Gulf and the twin bays of Vermilion and Cote Blanche, the shore of Louisiana becomes smooth and regular, curving gently in a shallow S to where it meets the Texas border at the mouth of the Sabine River system. A good part of this region consists of salt marshes. The low-lying land regions provide the conditions needed for growing rice.

In the far western corner of Louisiana, the swampland finally gives way to some stretches of firm beach. However, even here, the surface part of the beach is not the hard packed, pleasant one made of billions of quartz or coral sand grains, but is a distant relative of the swampland to the east. An example is Holly Beach, about 20 miles from the Texas border, whose topmost layer consists of several inches of black mud. The beach walker sinks into this slime with each step. There is very little temptation to lie down and get covered with the sticky oil-like substance.

Past the Sabine Pass, a short body of water connecting Sabine Lake (formed by the waters of the Sabine River) with the Gulf, the shore changes, as if to announce the crossing of the border from Louisiana to Texas. Instead of desolate-looking swamp, the coast behind the beaches becomes flat grassland, stretching to the north as far as the eye can see. Some of these stretches of grass are part of the large cattle ranches for which Texas has been long famous.

The beach sands seem firm and are pink or white rather than black. "Here and there along the lonesome beach," describes Leonard Ormerod in *The Curving Shore,* "groups of terns sit with their heads pointing into the breeze, dowitchers, sandpipers and other shore birds run along the edge of the surf, and farther out a brown pelican sails lazily above the dimpling water, into which he dives occasionally to capture a luckless fish."

These shore birds often gaze stolidly at large black tankers moving into the Sabine Pass from the Gulf. The tankers are heading for Port Arthur on Sabine Lake, the shipping point for the black gold delivered from the region where the first gushers in Texas oil history, those of Spindletop Field near Beaumont, were first brought in in 1901.

The sand fringe extends south-southwest until it curves down into a long thin peninsula that forms the eastern barrier between Galveston Bay and the Gulf. About a half mile across the bay inlet is the city of Galveston, located on the tip of a 30-mile-long sand island. The desolate shore of Galveston Island in 1528 was the point of arrival for several shipwrecked Spanish explorers, the first Europeans to land on the Texas coast. Their leader, Álvar Nuñez Cabeza de Vaca, called the island "Mal Hado," or island of ill fate.

The designation might not seem correct to a vacationer basking in the sun on the city's famous strip of tan colored sand. The water, warm as a bathtub on most days, moves lazily across the long sloping sea floor to break with only a slight flurry of white foam on the beach. During hurricane season, however, the wind and waves can be whipped into a roaring fury, so that they hit the exposed southern shore of the island like a battering ram. On September 8, 1900, such a combination of wind and wave resulted in a disaster that destroyed most of the city and killed an estimated 6,000 people before the waters receded. Since then, a huge sea wall has been built to prevent a recurrence.

Galveston, however, is the only major center directly fronting on the Gulf. Practically all of the coast of Texas is sheltered behind an almost continuous chain of long narrow sand islands. These islands were a result of countless years of wind and wave action on the silt brought down to the Gulf by the many small rivers that enter from Texas or by the longshore transport of some of the sand from the water-soaked Mississippi plain.

Today there are many port cities located in the bays and shallow inlets behind the island barriers. Most of these were made possible by decades of development by state and army engineers. The steady delivery of silt from inland regions had been contained within the harbor areas by the islands, which caused a buildup of the level of the subsurface soil. Decades of dredging were needed to remove this silt and provide harbors deep enough for large vessels.

The result has been the development of 25 new ports—12 deep-water ones and 13 able to handle barges and light draft vessels.

A major example is a city located up the bay from Galveston. This is Houston, number one port in Texas and now the control point for man's exploration of space from the National Aeronautics and Space Administration's Manned Space Flight Center.

Between the lower portion of Galveston Island and the marshy coast, the muddy water of West Bay makes its way. This stream meets the Gulf through narrow San Luis Pass, a waterway separating Galveston Island from the thin peninsula that stretches northeast from the mouth of the Brazos, a river famed in many a cowboy song. Starting some 15 miles below the Brazos Delta, another long sliver of sand, about 40 miles long, provides the lower border to Matagorda Bay. This bay is located approximately in the center of the Texas coastline, which measures about 367 miles from Louisiana to the Mexican border. (The total tidal shoreline is about 1,100 miles.) Beneath the mainland coast in this region were found some of the greatest deposits of sulphur in the world, and stockpiles of the bright yellow substance can be seen in numerous storage yards along the bay shores.

Matagorda Island, whose eastern tip forms one side of the entrance to Matagorda Bay, also touches on San Antonio Bay. Salt marshes stretch along the western border of this bay, and continue around part of the eastern shore of Aransas Bay. Aransas, whose waters are blocked off from the Gulf by St. Joseph Island, offers a

The white quartz sands of Padre Island (south tip of Padre in background) and Brazos Island form narrow bastions separating the mainland coast of south Texas from the Gulf.

Three man-made islands and their connecting causeways form a series of T-heads on the Corpus Christi waterfront.

variety of shore makeup along the remaining 25 to 30 miles. First the salt marshes taper off to be replaced by grassland dotted with mesquite trees and prickly pear. Then the soil behind the beach becomes rich and dark, providing a base for fields of cotton and grain. As the shore curves down to the town of Aransas Pass just before Corpus Christi harbor, the sand takes over again, this time bordered by strangely shaped live oaks.

The shoreline of Corpus Christi, bristling with tall, gleaming office buildings behind the long, stepped concrete buttress that extends to the edge of the water, would astound Alonzo Álvarez de Pineda, who named it in 1519. He would have found the region more familiar had he returned in the mid 1800s, for the city on the estuary of the Nueces River really did not begin to take shape until the 20th century.

The usually gentle waters of Corpus Christi Bay are separated from the Gulf by Padre Island, named after Padre Jose Baille, to whom it was granted in 1792 by King Charles IV of Spain. The island lies all the way across the direct entrance to Corpus Christi. The entry channel is found near Port Aransas between the tip of Padre Island and St. Joseph Island. Actually, this northern 20 miles of Padre is called Mustang Island on some maps. However, the white quartz sands that caused early Spanish explorers to call it Isla de Blanco have filled in the one-time gap between Mustang and its larger neighbor. The result is one of the oddest islands in the world.

Although it never gets more than four miles wide, Padre parallels the coast for 130 miles. Its white sand dunes, alternated in places with stretches of grassland, form a bastion from Port Aransas to the mouth of the Rio Grande. The narrow stretch of water between Padre and the mainland is called Laguna Madre. Its salt content, though, shows it to be a true part of the ocean. So is Baffin Bay, which juts westward into the mainland about 20 miles south of Corpus Christi. Samples of its water show it to be the third saltiest waterway in the world, following Israel's Dead Sea and Utah's Great Salt Lake.

The grass, cactus and mesquite along the southern banks of Baffin indicate that it is range country. And indeed, Baffin marks one of the boundaries of the famous King Ranch, the largest cattle ranch in the world.

The shore from Baffin to Port Isabel, the Gulf gateway for the city of Brownsville, is mostly a fringe of grassland behind long stretches of white sand. Here, as elsewhere on the Texas coast, a bird watcher would be rewarded with many unusual sights. Such striking specimens as the great blue heron, brown pelican, rare snowy egret and royal tern and the very rare whooping cranes find the region to their liking. The havens of the rarest of these, such as the cranes and egrets, are now sanctuaries. These include South Bird Island slightly north of Baffin in Laguna Madre and Laguna Atacosa. The latter is located 20 miles north of the point on the coast where the Rio Grande, forming the entire boundary between the Lone Star State and Mexico, completes its long voyage to the sea.

There is a great difference in geology along the Gulf coast. However, the intertidal life is

Shrimp boats are found plying their trade in all sections of the Gulf coast.

much the same throughout the region. The tie binding all the diverse land areas together, of course, is the Gulf of Mexico, whose warm waters wash the entire stretch of shore. Only small differences in temperature, salt content, etc., occur from one place to another.

From the standpoint of Gulf coast residents, by far the most important tidal dweller is the shrimp of the family *Peneidae.* The *Peneidae* are swimming shrimp, whose first three pairs of legs have small paddle-shaped extensions called *chelae.* The most numerous are the relatively large *Penaeus setiferus,* which live in middle and lower intertidal zones throughout the Gulf coast and up the Atlantic coast to Virginia. Two other types, the brown grooved shrimp and the pin grooved shrimp, are basically Gulf coast dwellers. (The large members of these species are called prawns, the smaller members, shrimp.)

As the thousands of small shrimp boats that berth at harbors all along the Gulf coast indicate, harvesting shrimp is one of the major economic factors in the region's economy. Several hundred million shrimp and prawns are taken every year from Gulf waters.

Close behind in importance is the oyster. Louisiana alone harvests 8,000,000 a year. The object of most of this human effort is the American oyster. Also making its home in the shallow sheltered waters along the Gulf is the thorny oyster. This member of the mollusk family gets its name from the small spines extending from the radiating ribs that ornament the outside of its red, white or purple shell.

Clams of many shapes and sizes burrow into the soft mud of many sections of the middle and upper intertidal zones. The one most sought as food is the *Venus mercenaria,* known by many pseudonyms including littleneck, hard-shell clam, Quahog, etc. Small white or purple beads cut from this clam's shell provided the Indians with the currency known as wampum. And frequently finding its way into the thick chowder of the southern states is the meat of the clam known as *Venus mortoni.*

Along rocky stretches of coast, many rock-boring mollusks make their homes. Many of the mollusks provide Gulf beaches with a source of beautifully shaped and colored shells. Not the least of these is the family of sunset shells. These grow shells with shining, translucent surfaces compared by experts to fine porcelain.

The arc family is also plentiful in the middle and low intertidal zones, as they are along the southern Atlantic coast. Most striking is Noah's Ark, whose wide gap along its mantle gives the appearance of the deck of a ship. Other arcs found from Texas to Florida include the Ponderosa Ark, with a heavy and greatly arched shell, and the American Ark, whose deeply ribbed shell has the look of a coolie hat when viewed from the side.

Crabs of many kinds make their way between the multicolored sponges, anemones and hydroids of the intertidal region. To name just a few, southern beaches are visited by such arthropods as the calico crab, the highly prized common blue crab, and the mud dwelling purplish- or brownish-red stone crab.

The intertidal life forms thrive in the comfortable Gulf waters, despite man's pollution here as elsewhere, with industrial waste. Many southern beaches are stained from time to time by patches of oil leaked from the growing string of offshore wells dotting the Gulf. But the ocean life, in general, seems unaffected. In fact, some of the best fishing in the teeming outer waters is near the floating derricks whose sea floor pilings seem to make pleasant homes for many members of the undersea animal communities.

Chapter 8

Land's End

FLORIDA IS THE only state with extensive shore lines fronting on two different major bodies of water. Its east coast is washed by the turbulent flow of the swift-moving Gulf Stream that forms a warm river in the ocean between the hard packed beaches and the deep, cold Atlantic. Its western shores slope gently into the more peaceful waters of the inland ocean arm called the Gulf of Mexico.

In overall climate, too, Florida shows a dual nature. Its position, slanting southward from the lower end of the East coast, places it within one degree of the tropics. It is, however, theoretically in the temperate zone and the northern part of the state reflects this with mild, but usually not excessively hot weather in summer and an occasional snowfall in winter. Because of the way the winds and sea currents meet over the lower half of the state, though, the climate here is subtropical. And many trees, plants and ocean dwellers are found here that relate closely to the life of the steaming equatorial regions.

From the air, the pointing finger of Florida is a patchwork of green foliage and myriad lakes and rivers. So numerous are its inland waters (including the second largest lake completely inside United States boundaries, Lake Okeechobee), that it seems more of the sea than the land. This, in fact, is a logical conclusion. For a good part of past ages up to a comparatively recent 10 or 20 million years ago, the land called Florida did not exist. If a time traveler could go back several hundred million years to the Paleozoic period, he would see the waters of this region stretched serenely across all of Florida's site, broken only here and there by a chain of volcanic islands connected at one end to the present Caribbean islands.

Over millions of years, the wind, rain and sea combined to grind away the peaks and deposit the sand grains in sediment beds around the islands. Adding to the sediments were the calcified remains of trillions upon trillions of sea animals, ancestors of the coral, snails and many other species. The added weight helped to force the islands, already receding beneath the waves, even deeper into the earth's crust. By the late Tertiary period, 12 to 28 million years ago, the limestone sediments were several thousand feet thick. The chemical reaction of the limestone deposits resulted in a structure that was not muddy or sandy, but a hard, rocky sea-floor plain.

By this time, the sea floor in this vicinity took the shape of a large, almost unbroken plateau. The change of forces in the earth's crust in the late Tertiary caused a great amount of pressure to build up under the center of this plateau. Nature, to gain relief from this tremendous strain, forced the central limestone section to arch upward until part of the plateau rose above the ocean waters into the light of day. Erosion soon set in to wear away the center of the arch. Meanwhile, the rivers from the land masses to the north cut their way through the limestone, depositing inland materials—phosphates, silts and clays—along many river banks and along the ocean shores.

The position of Florida's shores was far different in those ancient times than they are today. This was particularly true during the Ice Age when the slow progress of the polar cap toward the equator gobbled up much of the world's water and froze it in the form of snow masses or glaciers. The oozing ice frontier never reached Florida, but the withdrawal of water from the world ocean lowered the ocean level and exposed almost all of the Florida plateau to the sun's rays. The extension of the ice cap was not a constant one, but occurred in several cycles of expansion and contraction. Each of these caused a different level of water around the world and, thus, a different coastline for Florida. Today, with the ice cap back to its smallest size in billions of years, you might think Florida would be an ocean floor again. To some extent, this is so—about half of the plateau is underwater. Luckily, however, a combination of other subsurface forces have apparently raised the level of this huge limestone foundation so that it is able to withstand the sea's assaults of our present age.

This brief description of the formation of Florida helps explain why large sand deposits can be found in almost any region of the state. It does not explain the makeup of the underlying limestone rock, though. Some experts refer to Florida as a huge coral reef. Others deny it, noting that the basic material of the plateau is a substance called oolitic limestone. This limestone, however, can be made in several ways.

One way is purely chemical. The ocean contains large amounts of calcium carbonate. Under proper conditions, the sea water can become supersaturated with this substance, causing the calcium carbonate to precipitate out in the form of limestone. On the other hand, oolitic limestone can be formed from the remains of sea animals and, over countless periods of time, these can be amalgamated into a limestone so well mixed that it is not possible to tell what animals originally contributed to it or, indeed, whether it was made by this process or by chemical reaction.

In all probability, the bedrock of Florida was probably formed both by chemical and organic processes. As to the wide strands of beach that surround most of the peninsula's coastline, there is no such confusion. Geologists today have much less trouble in identifying the origins.

When Spanish explorer Ponce de Leon became the first white man to land on the region during Easter week of 1513, he probably was struck by the dazzling whiteness of the broad

Hurricanes may churn the Atlantic waters into monstrous battering rams at times, but most of the year the Florida shore reflects this mood of calmness and serenity.

sandy beach. Of course, he was more interested in finding the legendary Fountain of Youth believed to lie somewhere inland than studying the makeup of the shore. But even if he had this interest, there would have been little scientific knowledge to guide him to the present understanding that the beach along this northern part of Florida's east coast (between the present-day cities of Jacksonville and St. Augustine) was made mostly of quartz. In studies made mainly in this century, geologists have identified the beaches here as resulting in most part from sand carried to the shore by the rivers of Alabama and Georgia and by shore currents.

It was across these quartz boundaries that the expedition of Pedro Menéndez de Avilés marched to found the city of St. Augustine in 1565. The bulky fortress, topped by sawtooth walls to accommodate cannon or riflemen, still looks out to the deep blue waters of the Atlantic, just as it did after Menéndez' men built it. Standing today as well, are other buildings of the Spanish settlement, part of a picturesque city that is the oldest established settlement in the United States. It is not, however, the first settlement. Several abortive Spanish attempts were made in earlier years and, in 1564, French Huguenot colonists built Fort Caroline on the St. John's River some miles inland from the coast. The Spanish, however, did not want competition from other nationals, and troops from St. Augustine destroyed Ft. Caroline and killed most of its inhabitants in 1565.

Many cities and towns have grown up along the Florida shores in the hundreds of years since then. Despite this, the sweep of beaches running south from St. Augustine are relatively free of the overwhelming evidence of man's presence that occurs, for example, in southern California or the beaches of New York. The long, low barrier beach, separated in most places from the mainland by calm inland waterways, stretches off to the horizon with few obstructions. In some places, the quartz particles are loosely intermingled and give easily to any pressure. In other places, the beach sands are packed tightly and compactly together. One notable place where this occurs is Daytona Beach.

In the automotive world, the sands of Daytona are as renowned as the salt flats of Bonneville. Long before daredevil drivers fought the clock at speeds of hundreds of miles an hour in Utah, the first racing pioneers were competing along the several-mile-wide stretch of Daytona. In the early 1900s, some of the first builders of nationally known horseless buggies were engaging in challenge races here. The major stock car racing governing body, the National Association of Stock Car Auto Racing (NASCAR) was founded in Daytona in 1948 and still maintains its headquarters at the Daytona Beach Superspeedway.

Below Daytona, the barrier beach swings outward at a 45-degree angle to Cape Kennedy, then swings back toward the straight sweep of the mainland shore at Melbourne. This triangular section of land is composed of miles of grass-covered duneland segmented by many small streams and backed by a larger body of water called the Indian River. In Ponce de Leon's time, alligators roamed the waters and birds of brilliant plumage darted between the moss-covered trees and dense thickets that bordered the water between the otherwise desolate dunes. Today, the alligators are almost gone and the trees and bushes are dwarfed by high skeleton-like metal structures that point skyward along many parts of the Cape Kennedy triangle.

Here, among the sands of Florida's central east coast, the roar of the incoming sea is often drowned out by the shattering thunder of rockets carrying man out beyond the atmosphere toward the vast reaches of space. From just this stretch of shore, the bright yellow-red flame of Apollo 11 was reflected in the vibrating pool of water surrounding launch pad 39 on July 16, 1969. The grains of sand bounced momentarily in response to the forces generated by the engine that carried Neil Armstrong, Ed Aldrin and Mike Collins on their way to the waterless black sand surface of the moon.

Below Cape Kennedy, the ingredients in the shore begin to change. As we get closer to the tropics, the amount of quartz on the beach slowly lessens and the content from the ocean world goes up. More and more of the beaches come from the shells and shell fragments of untold generations of seashore dwellers. In the vicinity of the resort town of Palm Beach, over a third of the beach sands come from these remains. By the time the highly populated stretch from Ft. Lauderdale to Miami comes into view, the proportion of quartz has dropped to below 50 percent.

The shining, white, pink or turquoise high-rise hotels that line the pink-white sands of Miami

A diverse collection of bird species is to be found at the Cape Kennedy Space Center, where about half of the 88,000 acres are included in a wildlife refuge. Here, a great blue heron wanders unconcerned by rockets and missiles through a shallow branch of the Atlantic.

The hotels of Miami Beach tower above the coral sands of this barrier island—one of the most famous island cities in the world.

Beach look out upon the aquamarine waters of the Straits of Florida. The straits comprise a steep trough 434 miles long and 90 to 145 miles wide that separates the Florida continental shelf from the shallow Bahama Banks. Miami Beach is located on a long narrow sand island which is connected to the city of Miami by a series of causeways spanning the upper reaches of Biscayne Bay. This is the first of a series of islands, most of them built up from countless generations of coral animals, that swing in an arc beyond the tip of mainland Florida to Key West and the Marquesas Keys located about 160 miles due south of Ft. Myers.

The island of Miami Beach and the next few islands just north of it form the barrier that holds the full force of the ocean from 30-mile-long Biscayne Bay. The pink sands on the mainland shore of the bay are formed almost totally from the remains of the coral that long flourished in the shallow waters of the continental shelf in the region.

Not too far past the metropolitan area of Miami, the terrain and the mood of the region abruptly change. The settled, cosmopolitan north shore gives way to the mysterious, lonely region of marshland called the Everglades. Along the coast, behind the barriers of the keys, the calm waves of Florida Bay wash against shores pockmarked with watery indentations, hummocks of sandy mud and broad stretches of overhanging trees and vegetation. This northern tip of Florida, from Barnes Sound west to Cape Sable, then curving convexly north and west to Cape Romano, is one of the most unusual features of the shores of America and, indeed, of the world.

Between Barnes Sound, located just above Key Largo, and Cape Sable, the tides march against an army of great olive-leaved trees whose trunks are twisted and gnarled, like souls in torment. The roots of these trees go far into the ground and out along the shore for distances often as long as the tree is high. The tree roots mingle with those of bushes and flowers to form a thick mat that refuses to give way to the pounding of the sea. Indeed, the intertwining underground tendrils trap the sand and debris brought in by the water, slowly compiling it into new land and extending the shoreline southward.

To the west of the vast mangrove swamp, Cape Sable, with its wind-tossed sand dunes, comes into view. The northern tip of the three-pronged cape forms the lower part of the entry to Ponce de Leon Bay. Across from this point, the northern gate, Shark Point, is marked again by the tall, closely-packed stands of mangrove. From here over the 80 miles to Cape Romano, the shore is a continuously changing jumble of trees, sand and mud patches. The region is called Ten Thousand Islands and the chances are this figure is conservative. The islands are formed from sand dunes piled up over countless centuries by erosion and the action of hurricane winds on the long sloping plateau, now submerged, that once was land during some of the periods of the Ice Age. The base of the line of sand dunes was submerged when the receding ice cap freed billions of gallons of water.

Twisted branches, gnarled tree roots and undergrowth mingle with the incoming tides near the mouth of Florida's Everglades.

This long stretch of coast is the border of the swampland. Actually, this is a shallow river flowing from Lake Okeechobee down the gently tilted lower slope of Florida to the sea. It is a body of water approximately 100 miles long and from 50 to 70 miles wide. But it is not a free and open body of fresh water. Seen from the air, it is as green in many places as a forest. It seems to be water dissected by countless islands.

The greater part of these islands are not islands at all, but dense matted colonies of sharp pointed grass called saw grass. This grass has made the Everglades a green wilderness. Billions upon billions of its blades can germinate and grow in the water without ever touching soil. The combination of saw grass and water makes this a unique river, a stream sometimes called the "River of Grass."

The Everglades, a name apparently meaning ever-grassy river, has long been considered foreboding and dangerous. Tales sprang up about men wise in the ways of the vast marsh who disappeared without a trace. The Indians talked of spirits who lived in the untrackable wilderness. Some of these tales are only that; a few are true. It is also true that the Everglades holds a peculiar charm for anyone who loves the many faces of nature.

The mangrove-lined mouth of the Everglades accounts for only about 10 percent of the 770-mile-long Gulf coast of Florida. Above Cape Romano, this coast veers north and west in an uneven, often indented sweep that contrasts sharply with the almost straight-flowing lines of the Atlantic coast. Fronted by small low-lying islands much of the way, wide sand beaches are the order of things. They start just below the city of Ft. Myers, which guards the entrance to Charlotte Harbor, a drain for the Myakka and Peace Rivers. Above Charlotte Harbor, the barrier islands hug the coast past Sarasota and the twin cities of St. Petersburg and Tampa, whose buildings line much of the banks of Tampa Bay.

This region, which includes such other well-known towns as Clearwater, Bradenton and Tarpon Springs, is the second most densely populated part of the state, ranking just below greater Miami. But the milder weather—an average of 220 days of sunshine tempered by cooling breezes from the Gulf of Mexico—draws many senior citizens who are looking for a place of warmth and beauty to spend their retirement years. Many draw renewed vigor from the chance to bask in the sun while gazing over the usually calm, bright-blue waters of the Gulf. The fishing is excellent and the crystal-clear waters allow an undisturbed view of the varied life along the shallow floor of Florida's Blake Plateau. This plateau extends well over 100 miles out into the Gulf from almost all of the western shore of the Florida peninsula. Unlike the shores of the west coast, the offshore regions around the peninsula are smoothly sloping and free of submarine canyons. As a result, Florida does not lose much sand in its longshore currents to the ocean deeps.

Above St. Petersburg, the shore curves inward from Tarpon Springs past Chassahowitzka Bay and Wacassassa Bay to the mouth of the Suwannee River. The Suwannee, made everlastingly famous by the song of Stephen Foster, brings brown and red soil down from the hills of Georgia to mingle with the Gulf waters. Some of this is spread down to the south, piling up small quartz beaches against a shore that is, for the most part, marshland. Above the Suwannee, in the westward sweeping arc of Florida's panhandle (almost a single smooth curve except for the large bump of land pointing southward between Apalachee and St. Joseph Bays), the shore is again wide and sandy. The panhandle shore from Apalachicola to Pensacola near the Alabama state line is almost pure quartz, and comes from the same inland sources that provide the northern beaches of Florida's east coast.

The beach of the panhandle extends almost continuously for over 100 miles and seems as dazzlingly white as newly fallen snow. Wyatt Blassingame in *The First Book of Florida,* noted, "It glitters in the sun. It piles in huge, rolling, shifting dunes sometimes higher than a two-story house. Sometimes it looks like an arctic, snow covered landscape, except for the warm, blue-green gulf lapping against it."

The long stretch of Florida's coast, measuring 1,350 miles in general, or 300 miles longer than the California shore, is home for many kinds of ocean life. The total species probably is the most diverse of any section of the nation's coastlines. In numbers, too, a survey of tide or near-shore plants and animals would probably dwarf any other state's. It would be a backbreaking job to determine this, considering that the total tidal shoreline of the Peninsula State comes to almost 9,000 miles: 3,331 along the Atlantic and 5,095 along the Gulf coast.

The offshore waters of Florida form an ic-

A shrimp fisherman empties his haul off the panhandle coast of Florida.

thyologist's paradise. Over 700 different kinds of fish have been found here, the greatest variety anywhere in the United States. Fishermen cross the sand beaches of the state in record numbers almost every day to try for such prizes as tarpon, sailfish, perch, Spanish mackerel, pompano, grouper, gar, crappie, bluefish and sea trout. But an equally attractive lure can be found in the tide zones, where some of the world's largest concentrations of shrimp, crabs, crayfish, oysters, clams and scallops reside. Many of these sea animals are attractive delicacies for the state's shore bird families, also among the most varied in the nation and including such warmth-loving types as the snowy egret, pelican, ibis, heron and water turkey.

The shrimp colonies that can be found along the entire length of the coast are literally worth their weight in gold to commercial shrimp fishermen. The value of the shrimp harvest per year was over $20 million by 1970, roughly 20 times the state's income from lobsters and blue crab. Along the east coast, two types predominate—the white shrimp and the brown shrimp. Some pink shrimp are also found, though these are dominant along the Florida Bay and Gulf coasts.

Keeping the shrimp company in tide zones from low to high intertidal are many kinds of crabs and lobsters. The spiny lobster is often seen scuttling between the seaweed, the coral formations or beneath limestone outcroppings. The most common member of the lobster family in these waters, though, is the *Panulirus orgus,* which resembles the northern lobster but has a differently shaped shell and appendages. Along the southern shores of the state, a third lobster, *Panulirus guttatus,* makes its appearance.

Fiddler crabs, recognizable by the massive size of one claw, are present in all shore regions. These are sociable creatures, gathering together in huge cities beneath the sea floor. In some places, fiddler crab colonies may only total 100 animals or less, but in other places, underground settlements of thousands of the multiarmed crustaceans can be found.

The horseshoe crab makes his last stand in the peaceful bays and estuaries of the state, appearing in countless thousands in many areas. This crab was once common along the entire Atlantic coast, but it was considered a pest in some places and bounties of a cent a crab were paid for its destruction. Elsewhere, it was gathered indiscriminately to be ground for fertilizer. Recently, some of the wondrous talents of this tide dweller were reported by Dr. Talbot Waterman of Yale University. The horseshoe crab, he discovered, apparently can navigate successfully using just a small patch of blue sky to gain his bearings. He finds his way more efficiently and accurately than the best electronic aids used by jet planes.

In most of these waters, the Florida blue crab is a regular tenant. This crab is eagerly sought by commercial and amateur crabbers alike, who are well aware of the mouth-watering taste of its meat in any of 100 different food dishes.

It would take a catalogue as long as this book to detail the many forms of mollusk in Florida's

Though this looks like a flower garden, it is actually an oyster bed in Florida's Spring Warrior Creek.

waters. There are many types of limpet, scallops, the rock barnacle *Balanus,* the goose barnacle and several varieties of oyster. The oyster industry has long been a major one along the panhandle coast where, on calm days, fishermen by the hundreds can be seen manipulating long-handled rakes to harvest this sea-tide crop. On some beaches in the region, long high dunes of discarded oyster shells indicate that oystermen were there.

Off the southern part of the east coast, vast colonies of brilliantly colored coral animals live and die, contributing to the growth of beaches and land in their own way as their forebears did before them. A trip in a glass bottom boat skimming the crystal clear surface of these waters provides a view of these intricately shaped animals unmatched anywhere in the world. In the warm Gulf Stream waters, brilliantly colored tropical fish flash between the plant-like coral or the bulkier fronds of seaweed. Floating patches of sargassum, or gulfweed that fringe some of the coral gardens, remind the onlooker of the vast stretches of such weed in the Sargasso Sea.

In many places, the tidal zones shelter vast throngs of sponges. These primitive, simple animals have been harvested from Florida ports for many years. The sponge species are particularly plentiful off the west coast city of Tarpon Springs, which is why it has been given its title of sponge capital of the world.

No review of Florida's shores is complete without brief mention of the fierce looking inhabitants of some of its swamp inlets, the wild crocodile and the alligator. Like many forms of wild life, these legendary members of the lizard family are slowly being eliminated from their natural habitat by the inroads of man. Someday, their presence may be remembered only by the nickname of the University of Florida football team, the Gators, or the Jacksonville year-end classic, the Gator Bowl.

Index

INDEX
abalones, 36
Alabama, 129, 130. *See also* Gulf coast states
alligators, 170-171
Álvarez de Pineda, Alonzo, 145
anemones, 38, 55
animals, *see* life forms, shoreline
Aransas Bay, 143-145
arcs, 149
Atchafalaya River, 137
Atlantic City, 113
Atlantic coast, *see* central Atlantic states; Florida; New England

backshore, definition of, 14
Baffin Bay, 146
Baille, Padre Jose, 145
barnacles, 38
barrier islands, 62, 108, 109-111
bars, 7, 9, 17-18
   Ledbetter Point, 72
   see also spits
basalt, 64
Bascom, Willard, 6
bay-mouth bars, *see* spits
bayous, 137
beaches, 6-7, 10, 14
   California, northern, 50
   California, southern, 24-28
   central Atlantic states, 107, 108, 109-111
   flat, 72
   Florida, 64, 156, 157, 158, 160, 165
   formation of, 16-17
   Gulf coast states, 130, 140, 141
   New England, 82, 84
   Oregon-Washington, 60-64, 68, 69, 70
   summer vs. winter, 17-18
   types of, 62
   young, 62
   see also sand

bean clams, 38
berms, 7, 14, 16-17-18
Between Pacific Tides, 35
Bienville, Jean Baptiste le Moyne, sieur de, 129, 135
Biloxi, 132
Blassingame, Wyatt, 165
Borgne, Lake, 136
Boston Bay, 94
breakers, *see* waves
Burrell, Fred, 108
Buzzard's Bay, 97-98

Cabeza de Vaca, Álvar Nuñez, 141
Cabrillo, Juan Rodrigues, 45
California, northern (above Morro Bay)
   beaches, 50, 61
   California Cypress, 43
   climate, 50-51
   life forms, shoreline, 52-58
   Mendocino, Cape, 50
   Monterey, 43-45
   San Francisco Bay, 45-47
   sand, 50
   settlement, 43-45
   shore, description of, 41-43, 45, 47-51
   southern California comparisons, 41, 50, 51
   Tomales Bay, 49
   trees, 43, 51
   water temperature, 51-52
California, southern
   beaches, dangers to, 28-32
   beaches, formation of, 24-28
   canyons, submarine, 28-30
   climate, 50
   floods, 31
   grunion hunting, 40
   headlands, 23-25
   life forms, shoreline, 35-40
   Los Angeles, 23
   marshes and mudflats, acreage of, 22
   northern California comparisons, 41, 50, 51
   Pacific Missile Range, 24
   population growth, 20-23
   sand, 27-28, 30-32

settlement, 20-21
surfing, 34-35
California Current, 51
California mussels, 56-57
Calvin, Jack, 35
Cancer magister crabs, 77-79
canyons, submarine, 28-30
Cape Cod, 95-97
Cape Cod Bay, 95-97, 101
Cape Kennedy, 157, 158
Cape May, 113
Carmel, 42
Carson, Rachel, 109-110
Carter, Hodding, 133
central Atlantic states
 beaches, 107, 108, 109-111
 Continental Shelf, 107
 currents, tidal, 108-109
 Delaware, 114
 Delmarva Peninsula, 114
 Georgia, 121-122
 life forms, shoreline, 122-125
 Maryland, 114-116
 New Jersey, 111-114
 New York, 85, 111
 North Carolina, 116-119
 pollution, 106, 125
 sand, 109-110, 121-122
 settlement, 105-106, 117
 South Carolina, 119-121
 Virginia, 116-117
Cermeno, Sebastián Rodríguez, 46
Chignecto Bay, 89
chitons, 76
clams, 38, 58, 76, 79, 124, 149
Clark, William, 68
coastlines
 definition of, 14
 emerging and submerging, 60-61
 see also specific regions
Columbia River, 65, 68, 70-72
Connecticut, 100-101
Continental Shelf, 107
Cook, Captain James, 65
Coos Bay, 66
coquina clams, 124
coral, 55, 64, 170
coral beaches, 64
Corpus Christi, 145

crabs, 38, 55, 57, 77-79, 80, 122-124, 149, 168
crocodiles, 170-171
crust, earth's, movement of, 60-61
crustaceans, *see specific kind*
currents
 central Atlantic states, 108-109
 Humboldt Current, 51
 Japan Current, 51
 longshore, 12, 70
 riptide, 12-14
Curving Shore, The, 141
Cypress, California, 43

Daytona Beach, 157
Delaware, 114. *See also* central Atlantic states
Delaware River, 113-114
Delmarva Peninsula, 114
Disappointment, Cape, 68
Drake, Sir Francis, 45-46, 64
Dungeness crabs, 77-79
Duxbury Reef, 47

earth, movement of crust, 60-61
Eastport (Maine), 91
Edge of the Sea, The, 109-110
eel-grass, 58
Elizabeth Islands, 97
emerging coastlines, 60-61
erosion
 beaches formed by, 15-16
 during Ice Age, 82-84
 on Long Island (New York), 85
estuaries, 46
Everglades, 160-161, 163

face (of sea floor), definition of, 15
Fear, Cape, 119-120
Ferrelo, Bartolomé, 64
fiddler crabs, 168
First Book of Florida, The, 165
flood control
 California, southern, 31
 Oregon-Washington region, 62

floor, ocean, 28-30
Florida
  beaches, 64, 156, 157, 158, 160, 165
  climate, 151, 164
  Everglades, 160-161, 163
  geological formation, 152-154, 161
  life forms, shoreline, 165-171
  mangrove swamps, 161
  settlement, 154-156
  shore, description of, 151-153, 157-161, 163-165
Florida, Straits of, 160
foam, 9
foreshore, 14, 15, 17
Fort Caroline, 156
Fradkin, Philip, 22
Fundy, Bay of, 89

Galveston, 141-142
Georgia, 121-122. *See also* central Atlantic states
ghost crabs, 124
Golden Gate Bridge, 47
gravitational force, 89
Gray, Robert, 65, 69
Gray's Harbor, 69, 72
grunions, 40
Gulf Coast Country, 133
Gulf coast states
  Alabama, 129, 130
  beaches, 130, 140, 141
  life forms, shoreline, 148-149
  Louisiana, 135-140, 148
  Mississippi, 130-132
  pollution, 150
  settlement, 127-129, 135-136, 141-142
  shore, description of, 130, 133
  shoreline, extent of, 127
  Texas, 140-146
  see also Florida
Gulf Stream, 126

Hatteras, Cape, 117
headlands
  California, southern, 23-25
  effect of waves, 70

Heceta, Bruno, 64-65
Hedgpeth, Joel, 35, 47
Hermissenda crassicornis, 57
hermit crabs, 54-55
Holly Beach, 140
horseshoe crabs, 168
Houston, 143
Humboldt Bay, 46
Humboldt Current, 51
hydroids, 57-58

Iberville, Pierre le Moyne, sieur d', 129
Ice Age, 82-84, 85-87, 153, 161
ilmenite, 121, 122
Inman, Douglas L., 15, 32
Isles of Shoals, 93
isopods, 76

Jamestown (Virginia), 105-106
Japan Current, 51

La Jolla, 27
Laguna Madre, 146
Ledbetter Point, 72
Lewis, Captain Meriwether, 68
lice, rock, 54
life forms, shoreline
  adjustment to tides, 90-91
  California, northern, 52-58
  California, southern, 35-40
  central Atlantic states, 122-125
  Florida, 165-171
  Gulf coast states, 148-149
  New England, 102-104
  Oregon-Washington, 74-80
  Pacific vs. Atlantic, 36
  Puget Sound, 74, 76, 79-80
limestone, formation of, 154
limpets, 54
lobsters, 102, 167-168
Long Island, erosion of, 85
longshore currents, 12, 70
Lophopanopeus bellus, 80
Los Angeles, 23
Los Angeles River, 31

Louisiana, 135-140, 148. *See also* Gulf coast states

Maine, 87-93. *See also* New England
mangrove swamps, 161
Manhattan, 111
marshes
   California, southern, 22
   Louisiana, 139-140
   Maryland, 114-116. *See also* central Atlantic states
Massachusetts, 93-98. *See also* New England
Matagorda Bay, 143
Mendocino, Cape, 50
Menéndez de Avilés, Pedro, 156
Mexico, 127
Mexico, Gulf of, 126, 132, 137-139
Miami, 160
Michelson, Dr. Irving, 90
mid-Atlantic states, *see* central Atlantic states
Mississippi, 130-132. *See also* Gulf coast states
Mississippi River, 133-135, 137-139
Mobile, 129
mole crabs, 122-124
mollusks, *see specific kind*
Montauk Point lighthouse, 85
Monterey, 42-45
Monterey Peninsula, 40, 49
moon, gravitational force of, 89, 90
mudflats, southern California, 22
mussels, 56-57, 76
Myrtle Beach, 120

Nantucket Island tides, 101
Narragansett Bay, 98
neap tides, 90
New England
   beaches, 82, 84
   Connecticut, 100-101
   Ice Age, effect of, 82-84, 85-87

life forms, shoreline, 102-104
   Maine, 87-93
   Massachusetts, 94-98
   New Hampshire, 93-94
   Rhode Island, 98-100
   shore, description of, 82-85
   terrain, 81-82
   tides, 89, 91, 101
New Hampshire, 93-94. *See also* New England
New Jersey, 111-114. *See also* central Atlantic states
New Orleans, 135-136
New York
   Long Island, 85
   Manhattan, 111
   see also central Atlantic states
Newport, Captain Christopher, 106
Noah's Ark, 149
North Carolina, 116-119. *See also* central Atlantic states
nudibranches, 57

ocean
   canyons, 28-30
   layers, 52
   upwelling, 52
   see also currents; tides; waves
oceanography, 28
octopuses, 77
offshore, definition of, 14
oil, 139-140, 141, 150
Olympia oysters, 79-80
Olympic Mountains, 72-73
Oregon
   extent of shoreline, 66
   see also Oregon-Washington region
Oregon crabs, 80
Oregon-Washington region
   beaches, 60-64, 68, 69, 70
   climate, 65-66, 68
   Columbia River, 65, 68, 69-72
   Ledbetter Point, 72
   life forms, shoreline, 74-80
   Olympic Mountains, 72-73
   sand, 61-62, 64

settlement, 64-65
shore, description of, 59-60, 66-68, 72-73
organisms, see life forms, shoreline
Ormerod, Leonard, 141
oysters, 49, 77, 79-80, 148, 170

Pacific coast, see California, northern; California, southern; Oregon-Washington region
Pacific Missile Range, 24
Padre Island, 145-146
Passamaquoddy, 89
pecan trees, 130
Peneidae shrimp, 148
Perdido Bay, 130
periwinkles, 102
pill bugs, 76
plants
　Baffin Bay, 146
　eel-grass, 58
　Louisiana marshland, 139-140
　New England, 103
　sargassum (gulfweed), 170
　saw grass, 163
　see also trees
plunging waves, 34-35
Point Lobos, 43
pollution
　central Atlantic states, 106, 125
　Connecticut, 101
　Delaware River, 113-114
　effect on California mussels, 57
　effect on lobsters, 102
　Gulf coast, 150
　San Francisco Bay, 46-47
Ponce de Leon, 154-156
Pontchartrain, Lake, 136
population, coastline, 2-5. *See also specific regions*
Portland (Maine), 93
Portola, Gaspar de, 46
Puget Sound, 73
　life forms, shoreline, 74, 76, 79-80

quartz, 27

razor clams, 79
Redwoods, California, 51
refraction, wave, 69-70
regions, U.S., see California, northern; California, southern; central Atlantic states; Florida; Gulf coast states; New England; Oregon-Washington region
Rhode Island, 98-100. *See also* New England
Ricketts, Edward, 35
riptides, 12-14
"River of Grass," 163
Roanoke, 117
rock cockles, 79
rock lice, 54
rock oysters, 77
Rockaway Spit, 111
rough periwinkles, 102
rutile, 121-122

St. Augustine, 156
San Francisco, history of, 46
San Francisco Bay, 45-47
San Pablo Bay, 46
sand
　California, northern, 50
　California, southern, 27-28, 30-32
　central Atlantic states, 109-110, 121-122
　movement, 11-12, 14
　Oregon-Washington region, 61-62, 64
　types of, 64
　see also beaches
Sandy Hook, 111
Santa Barbara, 24-25
sargassum, 170
saw grass, 163
scallops, 80
sea pansies, 125
Seashore Life, 47
seastars, 37
shoreline, U.S.
　extent, 14
　population, 3
　see also specific regions

shrimps, 38, 56, 148, 167
Smith, Captain John, 84
snails, 37, 58
South Carolina, 119-121. *See also* central Atlantic states
southern California, *see* California, southern
spilling waves, 35
spits, 62, 69, 70
    Manhattan region, 111
    Massachusetts, 95
sponges, 170
spring tides, 90
starfish, 122
submarine canyons, 28-30
submerging coastlines, 60-61
sulphur, 143
sun, gravitational force of, 89-90
sunflower seastars, 37
sunset shells, 149
surf zone, 10-11. *See also* longshore currents
surfing, southern California, 34
Suwanee River, 164-165
swamps
    Everglades, 160-161, 163
    mangrove, 161

Tarpon Springs, 170
Ten Thousand Islands, 161-163
terraces, 15
Texas, 140-146. *See also* Gulf coast states
Thunder Hole, 91
tide pools, 42-43

tides, 11, 89-91, 101
Tomales Bay, 49
trees
    California Cypress, 43
    California Redwood, 51
    mangrove, 161
    pecan, 130
tunicates, golden star, 103

upwelling, 51-52

Ventura, 27-28
Vespucci, Amerigo, 127
Virginia, 116-117. *See also* central Atlantic states
Vizcaíno, Sebastián, 43

Washington
    extent of Pacific shore, 73
    see also Oregon-Washington region
Washington clams, 76
Waterman, Dr. Talbot, 168
waves, 7-10, 11
    angle of, 12
    effect on headlands, 70
    Pacific vs. Atlantic, 36
    plunging, 34-35
    refraction, 69-70
    spilling, 35
    summer vs. winter, 17-18
    surfing, 34-35
Waves and Beaches, 6
whelks, 124
Willipa Bay, 69, 72
worms, 56

Recommended Reading

Bascom, Willard. *Waves and Beaches, the Dynamics of the Ocean Surface.* Garden City, N.Y.: Anchor Books, Doubleday & Co., Inc. 1964.

Blassingame, Wyatt. *The First Book of Florida.* New York: Franklin Watts, Inc. 1963.

Carson, Rachel. *The Edge of the Sea.* New York: Houghton Mifflin Co. 1955.

Carter, Hodding. *Gulf Coast Country.* New York: Duell, Sloan & Pierce. 1951.

Douglas, Marjorie Stoneman. *The Everglades.* New York: Rinehart & Co. 1947.

Hedgpeth, Joel; Ricketts, Edward; Calvin, Jack. *Between Pacific Tides.* Stanford, California: Stanford University Press. 1968.

Hedgpeth, Joel. *Seashore Life of the San Francisco Bay Area and the Coast of Northern California.* Berkeley, California: University of California Press. 1967.

Michelson, Dr. Irving. "The Call of the Running Tide." *Engineering Opportunities,* Vol. 7, No. 7: pp. 16-19. July 1969.

Ormerud, Leonard. *The Curving Shore.* New York: Harper & Bros. 1957.

About the Author

Irwin Stambler received his degree in aeronautical engineering from New York University and worked for a number of years in the aviation industry. Combining his engineering knowledge and his writing ability, he began free-lance writing for magazines and eventually became the materials editor of *Space/Aeronautics,* a leading trade journal for the aviation and space industry. At present, he is Western Editor for *Industrial Research Magazine.* He has written a number of books on scientific subjects for young people and, in addition, a book for adults about undersea exploration. Mr. Stambler lives with his wife and four children in Beverly Hills, California.